I0762929
THIS BOOK
BELONGS TO:

The Smallest of Joys

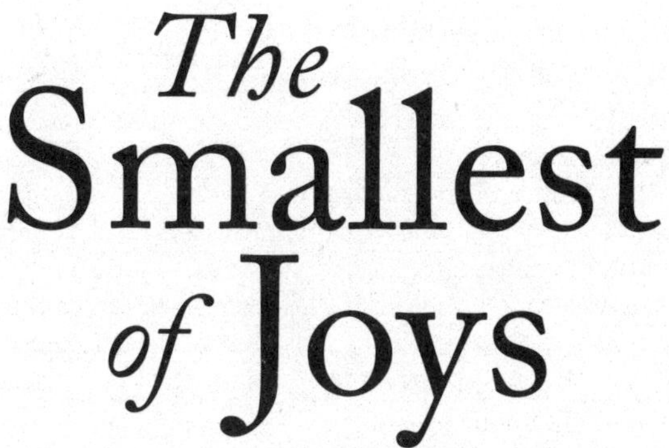

The Smallest of Joys

How to Create Your Own Magic, Let Your Best Be Enough & Find Contentment Exactly as You Are

DIANE SHIFFER

HAY HOUSE LLC
Carlsbad, California • New York City
London • Sydney • New Delhi

Published in the United States by: Hay House LLC, www.hayhouse.com®
P.O. Box 5100, Carlsbad, CA, 92018-5100

Cover design: Lisa Vega
Interior design: Claudine Mansour Design
Author photo: Photos by Bruce and Associates, Albion NY

Hardcover ISBN: 978-1-4019-9948-3
E-book ISBN: 978-1-4019-9949-0
Audiobook ISBN: 978-1-4019-9950-6

4th Printing

Printed in the United States of America

This product uses responsibly sourced papers, including recycled materials and materials from other controlled sources.

The authorized representative in the EU for product safety and compliance is Penguin Random House Ireland, Morrison Chambers, 32 Nassau Street, Dublin D02 YH68, Ireland. https://eu-contact.penguin.ie

For Millen . . .
my youngest daughter, my patient teacher,
my forever companion.

♥

Contents

Autumn 125

Winter 165

The Little Things

Sometimes it's the little things.

I've heard
that nature is good
for lifting one's spirits

and so
I'm taking my coffee
out to the front porch
this morning.

Oh, how I dearly love
my front porch!

There's sunlight
and a fresh breeze
and plants
and birdsong,

and I can feel
my whole self relaxing

and the joy seeping back.

And you know what I think?

It's almost always
the little things
that make
the biggest difference.

Dear Reader

Before I ever hit record, before the first video upload or caption or comment, I was already joyful. Not that joy had always come easily to me. After a lifetime of wrestling with anxiety and brushing up against the shadows of depression, I had slowly, gently taught myself how to notice joy. I was already confident in my small way . . . well, the kind of confidence you end up with after you've spent most of your life as a lovable oddball and finally decide to make peace with it. I delighted in beauty, treasured the domestic, and held kindness as a holy thing. I had a quiet little life, narrow in scope but rich in color and light. And I loved it.

But it never once occurred to me that anyone else might love it too.

I thought the world was looking for something flashier. I thought my patchwork days and threadbare ways were too quiet to matter. I knew there was pain and heartbreak in the world—I saw it everywhere—but it never crossed my mind that my small self might be able to offer any balm at all.

I had tricks and schemes for dealing with stress. I had "Sit and Stare Time" and little "Happy Traps" I set for myself, tucking tiny moments of joy into the folds of difficult days. But I never imagined anyone else would find them helpful. I certainly never imagined that sharing them might actually *matter.*

But then, my dear ones, you showed up.

You watched. You listened. You wrote to me.

You told me that these gentle things *did* matter. That my quiet life felt like home to you. That something in my voice, or my porch, or my jadeite cup full of coffee, or my cinnamon rolls had made you feel seen. Safe. Encouraged.

I thought I was giving something away, but it turns out, you were giving something back.

You showed me that kindness can stretch further than I thought. That vulnerability shared can bloom into strength. That the ache in someone's heart can soften, just a little, through the blue glow of a phone screen and a whispered "You matter."

You taught me to stand up to bullies. You taught me that standing up for the vulnerable can cost a great deal. And you taught me that it is *always* worth it.

Because of you, I've learned that my small life—this sedate, frivolous, cats-on-the-furniture kind of life—holds more than just my own joy. It holds a kind of quiet resonance that others can feel. A ripple that reaches further than I ever dreamed.

I may never meet many of you in person. But you are not abstract to me. You are not distant. You are *precious.*

And so, this book is my thank-you note. Thank you for showing me that what I have to give is enough. Thank you for receiving it so lovingly. Thank you for giving it back to me tenfold.

Thank you for rewriting parts of my story.

With all my heart,

Diane Shiffer

Introduction

This isn't a book about loud happiness or polished perfection. It is a book about moments, small ordinary moments that become joyful when we teach ourselves to notice. These smallest of joys, they've changed my life. And perhaps if we gather them together, they just might change yours too.

You know, I think joy sometimes gets a bit of a bad rap. Joy is seen as this magical, elusive thing that only deigns to visit on grand and glorious days: weddings, the birth of a child, that golden day when everything goes just right. We think it bubbles up unbidden and then disappears just as quickly, dissipating into the ordinariness of life. When the laundry piles up, when we spill that oh-so-necessary cup of coffee, when grief and loneliness seep into our empty hours, we might feel like joy has abandoned us entirely.

But joy hasn't left. She's just shyer than we expect. She waits patiently at the edges of our busy days, sending us pale little flickers to remind us she's still here: a sunbeam through the curtain, the warmth of something particularly yummy, a cool breeze arriving in the exact moment we need it most.

Joy asks us to slow down just enough to see her smiling from the corners, waiting for us to call her in. When we step into the busyness of our morning and pause to gaze at that sunbeam, to listen to the flutter of the curtain, to feel the breeze holding hands with her sister sunlight as they dance together through the window, we call joy in.

Those small, almost insignificant moments have power. They can warm our hands, brighten our faces, strengthen our hearts. They may seem fleeting, but they are not wasted. They can be fastened together like links of a chain. And isn't it true that the finest, most beautiful chain is made of the tiniest, most delicate links?

These joys, this quiet flickering beauty, must be protected, cherished. Carefully teased free of our distractions. Stored in the precious places of our hearts where they stay safe, ready for a dreary, ordinary hour, a dark, joyless day when we can pull them out and string the gently glittering joy-links around our necks. And let their beauty strengthen us for another day.

I actually didn't think I could ever write a book. I am in awe of authors who create characters out of whole cloth, writers like Tolkien or even Jill Barklem, who imagine whole new worlds and then put them down on paper so we can imagine them too. I can't do any of that. But I can make videos. I can create little collections of words and feelings to float over the tops of those images as voice-overs. So whenever anyone approached me about writing a book, I immediately declared my inability to do anything nearly so audacious . . . and in the process I convinced myself too!

So convinced was I, that I'm not sure why I agreed to speak with Allison Janice from Hay House. But I am so glad that I did. Allison listened so intently. She didn't agree or disagree with my insistences; she just gently asked questions. We talked about my process in creating videos, and it was Allison who first suggested I write a collection of essays. For the first time, I thought, *Yes, mayyyybe I could do that.* She suggested using my video scripts as starting points or inspiration, and I left that little chat not only thinking I might be able to write a book after all but feeling excited about the prospect.

I've always loved the passing of the seasons: summer into fall, winter into spring. My mood changes with the seasons. My energy level waxes and wanes with the weather. I am introspective and thoughtful in the winter, excited and full of ambition in the spring. Summer is joy. Fall is gratitude. So when it came time to organize this motley collection of essays into a book, we came upon the idea of gathering them up into seasons. The essays fell naturally into seasonal groupings just as my heart and mind fall naturally into their seasonal moods.

So I invite you to come along with me through the year. We can bolster each other in moments of struggle. Laugh together at the absurdity of life. Sit with me in fleeting moments of quiet. Join with me, my darling, join in my joy.

One tiny moment of joy can't change much. But even the very smallest of joys, all linked together, holding hands, moment by moment, day by day, year by year, can change a life. I know this, my darlings. Because they've changed mine.

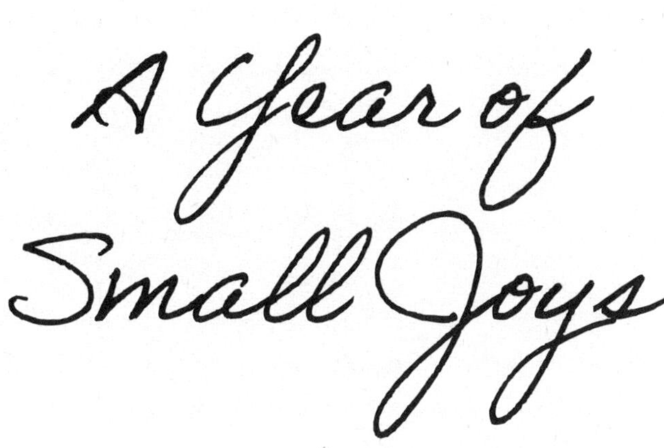

We are gathered here for a journey through an ordinary year made luminous by noticing. These aren't tales of grand adventures or glittering achievements but of the smallest treasures—quiet glimmers that steady us, delight us, carry us. Each season has its own character, its own rhythm, and its own invitation. Together, they remind us that joy doesn't have to be chased down; it's already here, waiting for us to pause, to notice, and to receive.

I Knew I Could Do It

Folks ask me all the time who helps me make my videos.

And the answer is simple: nobody. I do it all myself. The filming, the writing, the editing . . . every scene, every word. And I have so much fun doing it.

You see, even though I'm just a chubby old lady who never quite figured out how to use a digital camera, I somehow knew I could do this. There was this crazy, irrationally confident part of me that just knew. Knew I could connect with people in this medium. Knew I had something inside me worth creating. Something lovely, encouraging . . . and funny! Something that might make someone's day a little brighter.

Of course, not everyone shared that confidence. Most folks around me offered caution instead of encouragement. "The Internet's a rough place," they'd say. "You're going to get your feelings hurt." But one day, one person—just one—believed in me.

My dear friend Tara, who knows me well, looked me right in the eye over a Zoom chat and said, "I think you can do it. I really do. I think you could be very successful on social media. Just try it. Just start."

That one little spark of belief lit something in me. And so I tried.

It was kind of pathetic at first. I balanced my poor old iPhone 11 against a stack of books, hoping it wouldn't slip.

There's a particular magic in beginning something when you're not ready. In saying, "I'll figure it out as I go."

I pressed that little red record button and held my breath. I didn't know the first thing about editing or hooks or transitions. I only knew there was something inside me that wanted to be shared.

There's a particular magic in beginning something when you're not ready. In saying, "I'll figure it out as I go."

My first video was 17 seconds long: just a Mason jar of lavender lemonade sitting on my porch. It got 237 views, and I was ecstatic. My second video, a simple time-lapse of me doing my hair at my 1930s vanity, was the one that exploded. Millions of views. I was terrified but also delighted.

And then, almost by accident, I filmed the video that truly changed everything.

It was nothing fancy—just me wearing a cotton dress with lace-trimmed bloomers, hair piled into a bun, pumpkins scattered around me. I was sitting on my porch in the soft light of early autumn, offering a cinnamon roll and a warm welcome.

"Oh, my gracious," I said to the camera. "Come on up here. Sit in this chair . . . it's the most comfortable. I've added a little pumpkin spice to my cinnamon rolls, and I'd like your opinion. Help yourself to cream and sugar."

That was it. No trendy audio, no clever effects. Just a cozy moment, a plate of cinnamon rolls, and an invitation to be seen.

I didn't expect the response. The comments flooded in. Not just compliments on my dress or my pumpkins, but something far deeper. People said it made them feel loved. People who had been rejected, people who never knew a grandparent's warmth, people who had been told they weren't enough. Somehow, this little video, just a minute or two of soft words, spoke to them. Made them feel safe.

That's when I realized something important: It wasn't the vintage décor that mattered most. It wasn't the perfect setting or the polished script. It was kindness. It was gentleness. It was the invitation to sit down and be exactly who you are.

They weren't staying for the jadeite. They were staying for the kindness.

And I thought, *Kindness is something I can do. And not just* can *do.* Must *do.*

From that day on, I knew why I was on social media. My old linens, my vintage dresses, my quirky little kitchen trinkets: Those are just the backdrop. My real message is kindness.

Every clip I make, every caption I write, every quiet video of me folding laundry or pouring tea is just another way of whispering, *You matter. You are worthy. You are welcome here.*

I wanted to create beauty, yes: to make videos that felt like art, something quiet and unusual and warm. But more than that, I wanted to create a space where kindness is the main character.

And here's the thing I've learned: Sometimes what people need isn't instruction or advice. It's encouragement. One kind word. One gentle nudge. One person saying, "I see you, and I believe in you."

One kind word, one gentle nudge of encouragement, can go farther than we ever imagined. It can settle in someone's heart like a seed. It can bloom when they need it most.

So why do I make these videos? Because kindness was something I needed once, and now it's something I can give. What a beautiful, healing thing that is, giving what you once needed.

And now I turn this outward, to you, my dear one.

I bet there's something you know you can do, even if no one else sees it yet. Or maybe there's something that feels too far away to even dream. Let me be the voice that says you can dream it. You can do it. Try. Just try.

Because you never know what that first shaky step might lead to.

The world is aching for tenderness. And you never know how far one small act of belief might travel. Go ahead and give it. Share what you once needed. And don't be surprised if it begins to heal *you* too.

The Tiny Joys of the Unconventional Life

There is a quiet kind of magic in choosing to live differently. Not loudly. Not rebelliously. Just intentionally, thoughtfully. In ways that might make others raise an eyebrow but make you feel like yourself.

I'm not quite sure what first drew me to all things vintage. I think part of it came from a little storybook from my father's childhood, with two little girls drawn in glorious 1930s-style illustrations. I'm sure part of it came from my beloved Nana and her impeccable handmade wardrobe: thick woolen skirts, cashmere sweaters, pearls, silk dresses, and those spotless cotton aprons worn only inside the house. And I know, without question, that my obsession with household linens was born in dusty church basements of the 1970s and '80s—rummage sales with tables piled high with embroidered dresser scarves, lace doilies, and printed tablecloths (with matching napkins, oh joy!). No one else wanted the dowdy, out-of-style things . . . but I did. Oh yes, I *did*. I'd come home with bags of them, purchased for a pittance, delighted beyond measure.

Over time, my home filled with these treasures, often used in rather unconventional ways: tablecloths draped over worn living room furniture, doilies and antimacassars strung like banners, napkins as makeshift bookshelf curtains, quilts hung as drapes in the living room. For years, my vintage clothes mostly stayed tucked in the closet, only pulled out so I could breathe in their fragrance or admire a hemline. Sometimes I'd slip one on, twirl a little, and imagine what my Nana would say about the fit of a bodice or the drape of a skirt.

Eventually, though, I stopped saving them for "special" moments and began wearing them every day. And yes, to many, I looked odd . . . because really, my dears, isn't it peculiar to wear hundred-year-old clothes that once belonged to goodness-knows-who? But I didn't care. The comfort of finding what you love and being your whole self is such a joy that looking odd is a very small price to pay.

Like drinking coffee from a century-old cup on the most ordinary morning. Lining your drawers with lavender paper, even if no one else notices. Setting the table with embroidered napkins when you're only eating toast. Wearing your grandmother's brooch with your hoodie. Talking to birds. Naming your favorite tree. Watching old black-and-white films while soaking in the bath.

These aren't grand gestures. They're quiet ones. But they anchor you to joy. They remind you who you are.

A life full of these small odd joys might look eccentric from the outside. But from the inside? It feels like peace. Like home. It feels like choosing beauty over boredom, wonder over worry, delight over duty. And when others glimpse it—the doilies hung like banners, the perfume dabbed on before doing dishes, the quilts pressed into service as drapes—some will laugh. Some will shake their heads. But some will smile. And a few will understand completely.

You don't need to explain yourself to everyone. You only need to belong to yourself. And these funny little preferences, these sparkling rituals, are proof that your life is yours and that you are allowed to love it.

So go ahead. Be peculiar. Be particular. Be joyfully odd. Lay out your clothes the night before, even if you have nowhere to go. Hum while you dust. Stop in the middle of a Tuesday afternoon just to watch the sunbeams travel across your shiny living room floors. Keep your aprons starched. Drink your tea from china cups. Let your life be full of tiny joys no one else needs to understand.

Because they aren't frivolous. They are sacred. And they are yours.

One Small Moment

It can be hard to find our joy, to recognize those things that give us joy. Not the big, lavish, joyful days like weddings or the birth of a child or falling in love. Those are easy to spot. But for some of us, it's much harder to notice those quiet moments when joy almost slips past you and catches you unawares. When the eyes of your soul open wide, when you feel peace and excitement at hope, all one right on top of the other. It might only last an instant, but oh, how glorious it is while that instant lasts. And oh, how in the next instant, we forget.

Joy can be so fleeting that we almost miss it. The heaviness of depression can dull it, heartbreak can smother it, and soon we find ourselves living under a gray sky that feels endless. That cloud settles in so quietly, so gradually, that we stop noticing its weight . . . until it feels like the only weather we know. In those seasons, we can begin to believe that light isn't meant for us at all, that gladness belongs to other people but not to us. And that, perhaps, is the hardest part: not the absence of delight itself but the way it convinces us that we aren't even entitled to joy. But joy is always there, stubbornly waiting for us to call her out of the corners, to celebrate her, and to thank her for lightening our load and brightening our darkest days.

So here's a gentle invitation, my darling: Today, seek out one small moment of joy. Just one. Maybe it's a raindrop on your window, a flower blooming against all odds. An unexpected smile, a funny noise from your cat, a hot mug warming your hands. When it finds you, don't let it slip away unnoticed.

Make a note of it, write it down in a little joy journal, snap a photo, and save it in a special joy folder on your phone. Call a friend and share it aloud. Maybe even post it on social media, if you'd like. Send your delight out into the world. And let someone else catch a bit of your joy in their day.

Just one moment noticed and cherished. Let that be enough. Let that be everything.

Care for Yourself Like a Lace Doily

Years ago, my son Noah rescued an old lace doily from someone's trash heap. It was mildewed and stained, knotted up on itself like the little forgotten scrap that it was. Most people wouldn't have given a second glance, but Noah did, and he brought it home to me. I spent hours—days, really—offering it the gentlest, most persistent kind of attention. I soaked it in cool water, rinsed and re-rinsed it until the stain softened and the knots loosened. Eventually that delicate little scrap of lace returned to something close to its former glory.

Even now, all these years later, the doily requires special care. I hand-wash it in tepid water with a gentle cleanser, then roll it in linen to dry. It is starched and pressed with a careful hand. It takes time, it takes effort, but it is worth it. Because precious things deserve to be cherished. They deserve love. They deserve kind attention.

And so do you.

For most of my life, I felt guilty treating myself with the same care I so readily gave others. If there was something beautiful or special, I gave it to someone I loved. I made sure my daughter Millen had the cutest, most delightful things, the comfiest pajamas, the softest sweaters, the prettiest little notebooks. And me, I would wait. Wait until the dress I loved was on deep clearance. Wait until I could find something secondhand.

Not that there's anything wrong with secondhand, of course. Most of my favorite things have been loved many times before they made their way to me. But the pattern of it was telling. I believed I had to earn tenderness. I believed I had to justify joy.

Somewhere along the way, I began to understand just how wrong that was. An important part of caring for ourselves is treating ourselves with the same kindness we show to our most beloved ones, not only in emergencies or when we finally earn it, but as a regular, everyday act of love.

Because cruelty and neglect are never okay, not even when directed at ourselves.

We tell ourselves we can bully our way to self-improvement. We punish ourselves into better behavior. We think that if we deprive ourselves enough, we'll finally become good enough. But deprivation rarely leads to growth. But love does. Safety does. Nourishment does.

If you're making sure that others have nice things, it's okay for you to have them too. If you're working hard to keep others safe and happy, don't forget that your safety and happiness matter just as much. If you're loving others well, then please, my darling, make sure you're loving yourself too.

You're not too *this* or not enough *that*. You're not a misfit piece. You are a rare treasure with a shape all your own. You are not a scrap to be tossed aside. You are precious.

And precious things need special care.

So give yourself love, give yourself softness, give yourself the patience and gentleness you so freely give to others.

You deserve it. (Of course you do!)

You're not too this
or not enough that.
You're not a misfit piece.
You are a rare treasure
with a shape all your
own. You are not a
scrap to be tossed aside.
You are precious.

Happy Traps

Years ago, when anxiety and depression were my daily companions, I started setting what I called Happy Traps—small surprises, intentionally placed moments of delight to help Future Me get through hard days.

When I dreaded a meeting ahead at work, I'd queue up a favorite comfort show before I left in the morning so I'd know it was waiting for me when I got home. I'd order a silly little treat online just for the anticipation of its arrival, then wrap it up like a present and leave it on my pillow. I'd do my hair not to impress anyone but for the simple joy of brushing it out. I can't tell you how many dreary mornings were made bearable by the prospect of a curl and a bobby pin placed exactly right.

Happy Traps are not frivolous. They're gentle interrupters of pain. They're little breaths of fresh air that remind us joy still exists, even when the world feels bleak.

You can make one by stashing a piece of your favorite candy in the glove box of your car, then forgetting it on purpose so you can find it later.

You can set a slideshow of your children's bright eyes and soft hair or your cat's damp pink nose as your phone's lock screen. If 3:00 P.M. is always hard, coordinate with a friend to send each other encouraging messages or ridiculous memes right at that moment. Every day.

Happy Traps don't have to cost money or take time. They can be small comforts. A favorite mug rinsed and ready for your morning coffee. A spritz of the perfume that makes you feel outrageous. A sticker on the bathroom window that says you're doing just fine, my darling.

The truth is, hard seasons can make us forget who we are. We can get so wrapped up in surviving that we stop noticing the things that make us smile, that make us want to live. That's why Happy Traps matter. They reconnect us with the parts of ourselves that are playful and tender. They press pause on the cycle of despair and remind us that joy is still available, still real, still ours.

So if life feels heavy right now, I want you to know it's okay to delight yourself. It's okay to do small, silly things that make you feel better. It's okay to rig your day for happiness.

Go set a Happy Trap, darling, and then walk right into it with open arms.

A Guide to Setting Happy Traps

Happy Traps are little gifts to yourself. Pleasant little things. Tiny benevolent tricks for setting joy in your own path for yourself. They are sweet surprises you prepare for yourself, a gentle kind of trickery meant to coax a smile on a hard day or give your weary spirit something kind to land on. Creating Happy Traps isn't about buying expensive treats or curating someone else's idea of the perfect lifestyle. It's about tuning in to what makes you feel light and warm and quietly delighted. What gives you relief from the stress or the boredom or the heartbreak or whatever it is that is blocking your own joy? *Do that.*

Happy Traps are not just for times of crisis. It's not only folks who struggle with depression or anxiety who need Happy Traps. Most of us, even on our best days, can grow weary of the same old routines. We get a little tired, a little uninspired. Life can feel a bit too gray, a bit too ordinary. Everyone can use a sparkle of joy now and then, a moment that glows like morning sunlight through stained glass and sets bright-colored beams dancing across your otherwise boring furniture.

Here are some gentle ideas to help you set your own Happy Traps:

- **Stash treats in surprising places.** Place a tiny treat into the thumb of your mitten to sweeten a cold morning. Tuck a funny little charm into your coat pocket. Hide a little encouraging note in a drawer you use often. Let yourself forget, then be delighted when you stumble across it later, like discovering a love note left by your past self. Who knew?

- **Create a joyful folder.** Start a folder on your phone with photos that lift your spirits. A ridiculous close-up of your cat with the tip of her tongue sticking out. A screenshot of a kind text or video that always makes you laugh. Visit it when you're weary, my dear one. Let your joy collection be a balm.
- **Build in rituals to look forward to.** Make 3:00 P.M. your official "cocoa with whipped cream" time. Declare Friday morning Fancy Sock Day. Schedule a regular chat with a dear friend or a silly meme exchange at the exact moment your spirits tend to sag. Let your days have bookmarks of gladness.
- **Send yourself something lovely.** Order a small gift, a book, a candle, or a pair of earrings, and forget about it until it arrives. Wrap it up when it comes and give it to yourself properly: Sign it "To me" or "With love, from me" and definitely "with love." Sign it as if you're giving a present across time from a hopeful you to a future you in need of a smile.
- **Make a space that smiles back.** Pin a cheerful vintage hanky over a lampshade. Swap out your pillowcase for the one with the embroidered bluebirds. Put a stained-glass

rainbow in your window. Prop your favorite old stuffed teddy bear in a place of honor. Let your home wink at you with comfort and delight and humor. Let each corner whisper, "I'm glad you're here."

- **Keep a pretty project just for you.** Set out a jigsaw puzzle on a table by a window in a patch of sunlight. Stash a pile of fabric scraps for patching an old pair of jeans. Start knitting a scarf in your favorite color, and let it grow impossibly, hilariously long. Carry a coloring book and sharp new pencils in your tote. Not something you have to do, something you *get* to do. Something your hands can fall into while your thoughts drift like snowflakes in a globe.

The loveliest thing about Happy Traps is that they are never wasted. Even if you don't need them the day you set them, they'll be waiting quietly and kindly until you do, like a cat curled on a window ledge, like a bright bloom in a forgotten corner of your garden, just waiting for you to notice.

So go ahead, lay the trap, let it catch you when you fall.

Sit and Stare Time

I want to introduce you to one of my favorite things. I call it Sit and Stare Time.

Each morning, I make myself something delicious and caffeinated (usually nice hot coffee, sometimes iced, occasionally tea), and then I find myself a comfy lovely spot, a corner bathed in soft morning light, a patch of sun on the porch, a cozy chair by the window. And for a few blessed moments, I just sit and sip and stare.

Everyone needs a little Sit and Stare time in their lives. Back when I was a young mom, there was a lot of pressure to get up very early in the morning for Bible study and prayer. It was called quiet time, but it was often anything but quiet. It usually involved reading multiple passages across various parts of the Bible, following a study curriculum, praying for extended periods, engaging in self-examination, sometimes journaling, and always—*always*—taking notes.

I tried. I really did. But the truth is I always did better with study later in the day. And during those early mornings when I was still groggy and stretched thin, I often found myself just sitting and staring blankly into space. My eyes gravitated toward beauty. My heart settled into a quiet peace when I stopped trying so hard, and I simply allowed myself to be still. To sit in appreciation. To rest in gratitude.

In a rueful attempt at self-deprecating humor, I began calling it my "Sit and Stare Time." At first it was a little joke at the expense of my own raging ADHD, a way to laugh at what felt like lack of discipline. But over time I began to see the beauty in it. The benefit of unashamedly taking a few quiet moments at the beginning of the day, not to study or produce or reflect deeply but simply to be. Bible study is good. Prayer is healing and beautiful. But we don't have to be productive every minute, my darlings. We also need beauty. We need peace. We need joy. And sometimes we just need to sit down with a warm cup of something and stare out the window for a while.

I remember the rainy, difficult morning when I first realized the power of my silly little Sit and Stare Time. I had just gotten all my children where they needed to be. My oldest was very anxious about the school day ahead, and my youngest was sobbing at day care drop-off. I felt heavy with the weight of their needs and painfully aware of my own inadequacies. I wanted to be with them. My heart longed for the quiet of my simple little home. But work was a necessity, of course, and I made it there with a few blessed minutes to spare. Instead of rushing into the office, I lingered in my car. I held my drive-through coffee (hazelnut with two glorious helpings of cream) and felt its warmth through the paper cup. There was rain that morning, and I watched the drops of water migrate down the curve of the windshield. They joined into little streams and then just as quickly separated again into single drops. I breathed in the steam from my coffee. I gathered myself around the warmth of that silly little paper cup, and it shielded me.

The rain was beautiful. The quiet was healing. And in that moment, I realized comfort and beauty are everywhere. They're all around us, if we can somehow pause in the midst of the busyness, of the tension. If we stop long enough to look. If we accept that beauty can be small . . . small but never insignificant.

Isn't it odd how we allow ourselves to be pressured into doing things that make no sense for us personally? That don't fit our temperament or our rhythm or the particular season we're living in? I'm so thankful to be free of those silly little oppressions now. I'm so grateful to have let go of that inner voice insisting that rest must always be earned.

Years ago, my mornings were frantic, full of noise and rush. I had five little ones to get up and ready: day care drop-off, school buses, packed lunches, signed permission slips, all before I had to be at my desk by 7:30 A.M. I was tired. I was overwhelmed. And I was doing my best. Back then, Sit and Stare Time was my tiny act of rebellion and self-care. A sliver of peace before the day began. I'd steal a moment in the kitchen or on the porch, coffee in hand, and focus on one lovely thing. The light hitting a glass. The steam curling from my mug. The hush of a still house before it woke. That quiet moment sustained me through some very hard days.

These days, life moves more slowly. My mornings are quiet and full of pleasant little tasks. The coffee brews while the birds wake up. I open a window. I watch the light change. I still make time to sit with my coffee and notice one small bit of beauty—and my heart, without fail, fills with gratitude. That gratitude sustains me.

If your life right now is hectic and full of stress, I see you. I remember. I know how heavy that can feel. But please know this, my dear one: No season lasts forever. The challenges and heartaches of today will pass. And tomorrow? Tomorrow will have its own joys and beauties waiting for you.

If you're walking through a difficult time just now, take heart. Even now, even here, you can find one moment of peace. A small breath of stillness. Let yourself have that. Sit. Stare. Sip something warm. Let your heart rest, even if just for a minute.

Difficult seasons end, my dear. And there is always hope for the future.

Sit and Stare Time: A Reflection

Some mornings, the very best thing you can do is nothing at all, just for a moment. Sit and Stare Time is not fancy, it's not productive, but it's grounding and beautiful.

Sometimes I sit with my first cup of coffee and let my eyes drift toward whatever catches the light just right: the tulips my son Noah brought me arching gently in a little ceramic pitcher or the postcard of an Irish countryside scene that reminds me my daughter, who lives in Ireland, is on her way. A favorite teacup, yellow and bright as a marigold. Some days I marvel at the water cascading over the green leaves of my geranium as I water it or the snow drifting slowly past the window or the quiet, steady gaze of my black-and-white kitty.

That's it, that's all. Just stop for a moment, my darling, and look for something beautiful.

In years past, it was drive-through coffee in a paper cup on the way to a job I dreaded, and the beauty was harder to find, but even then, there was something. The warmth of the cup in my hands, the glistening of raindrops on the windshield. Wherever you are, whatever your morning looks like, I hope you'll give yourself a moment to sit and stare. Just one tiny minute to notice something lovely. Let that loveliness hearten you and give you strength for the day to come.

Meeting Fear with Joy

Are there things you're afraid of? Things you know you need to do, but you're almost paralyzed by dread? They might be simple, ordinary things to most folks: making a call, filling out that paperwork, checking the overdue balance on that loan. But they're not ordinary to you. You find yourself imagining the worst-case scenario and filling your heart with anxiety.

True confession, my dear one: that was me not long ago. I knew something wasn't right, and I needed medical testing. But I was afraid. I avoided it. I let my imagination run wild. And when I finally did move forward, the news at first wasn't good. The tests that were supposed to rule things out and set my mind at rest only created more cause for concern. But I kept going: through the fear, through the appointments and the waiting and the worry. I had procedures, followed by times of rest and healing. Doctor's visits where hopes for good news were dashed and more procedures were scheduled. Eventually, though, I had my last procedure. I took my last dose of medication. I put away the bandages, and I felt better. Gradually, day by day, I got better.

And now? Now the sun is bright, the sky is clear. I am filled with joy and surrounded by love. And I keep thinking: *What if I had let fear keep me frozen*?

Everything I wanted was on the other side of that fear.

I've learned that the only way out is through. Not around. Not under. Not tucked quietly in the back of your mind while you pretend it's not there. *Through.* Step by trembling step.

There was a time I wanted to avoid it all. And I did, for a while. But avoidance didn't bring peace. Courage did.

And here's what I want to tell you, dear one: Maybe your fear isn't big or dramatic. Maybe it's a tiny thing with heavy weight. A long-postponed phone call. A difficult conversation. A truth you don't want to face. Maybe it's simply admitting that something needs to change.

Whatever it is, I promise you: what you long for may be waiting just beyond it.

Be brave, my dear. Invite courage to walk with you. Invite joy to keep you company.

The way may be hard. But you won't be walking it alone.

And joy is still ahead.

She's waiting to be found.

How to Build a Joy-Filled Life

(According to a Slightly Eccentric Vintage-Loving Lady)

- **Collect delight like vintage buttons.** Tiny things matter. The glint of a teaspoon in sunlight. A cat's contented sigh. A perfectly ripe plum. The little moments are where joy hides.
- **Make peace with the fact that not everyone will get it.** You don't need universal approval. Some people just don't understand why anyone would find comfort in a threadbare apron or a chipped teacup. Love your things anyway. Love your *self* anyway.
- **Let joy be inconvenient.** Stop mid-task to admire the light filtering through lace curtains. Rearrange your whole afternoon just to see a friend's face. Bake a cake at 9 P.M. because you want to. Spontaneity counts.
- **Create rituals from the ordinary.** Light a candle before washing dishes. Sing while folding laundry. Make a ceremony out of your morning coffee. Ritual turns routine into reverence.
- **Wear what feels like you.** Even if it's not in style. Even if it's eccentric. *Especially* if it's

eccentric. The more yourself you are, the more joy has room to breathe.

- **Name the moments that feel good.** Say them aloud. Whisper them to yourself. Write them down. *This, right now, is good. This is joy.* Let yourself notice it.
- **Build little altars to joy.** A shelf with your favorite books. A bowl of lemon drops. A postcard that makes you smile every time you see it. Your beloved old doll dressed beautifully in spite of her tatty hair and permanently smudged nose. Make your space a haven.
- **Keep something just for you.** A drawer full of pressed flowers. A playlist that always lifts your spirits. A secret dance in the kitchen when no one's watching. Not everything needs to be shared to be real.
- **Find your people—or become someone else's person.** Be the person who sees the magic in others. Who celebrates their quirks. Who says, "Oh, I love how you do that!"
- **Allow yourself to be moved.** By music, by art, by a child's laughter, by the smell of old books. Let the beauty of this world get under your skin.
- **Forgive yourself for needing joy.** Joy isn't frivolous. It's necessary. Especially when things are hard. Especially when they don't make sense.

- **Be tender with the old you.** The awkward one. The one who tried too hard or not enough. She got you here. She deserves a cookie with her morning coffee and a thank you.
- **Trust joy to return.** Even if it leaves for a while. Even if the sky feels gray and your bones feel heavy. Joy is patient. She'll find her way back to you.
- **Choose joy—again and again.** Not because life is always sweet. But because *you* are. And your sweet soul deserves joy like flowers deserve rain.

This and That

On my social media, you'll see a lot of things that might seem familiar.

Me, in a 1940s cotton housedress, answering a rotary phone. A tidy room with sun-washed curtains and a cat perched on a cloth-covered table. Me, baking bread or a towering chocolate cake, hanging linens on the line, walking a country lane framed in blossoms. You'll see woolen bonnets, old cookbooks, dusty vintage catalogs, and long rambling chats over warm cups of tea.

And also: support for gender-affirming care. Black Lives Matter. Voting for a woman president (twice). Welcoming immigrants. Respect for other religions. Antifascism. Gratitude for modern medicine. Sustainable living. And honest conversations about mental health.

You'll see my child in an apron, potting plants on an old pink-and-green dresser drawer full of soil. You'll see cats—lots of cats. On the porch, on the furniture, on the dining table. You'll see me baking but also grabbing take-out tacos on a Tuesday. You'll see candlelit Advent spirals but also hear me celebrating others' sacred traditions.

All of this is me. This *and* that. The softness and the strength. The nostalgia and the progress. The faded, soft cotton quilt and a backbone of steel.

Many people find their way to me through the warm, old-fashioned aesthetic. The coziness. The sweetness. The Nana vibes. Some of those same people are surprised to find the values that live here too.

And I get it. It's not what you might expect. But the truth is, kindness without justice is just sentiment. Warmth without welcome is just decoration.

So here in my little corner, we hold space for both. We bake the bread *and* make space at the table. We hang the laundry *and* challenge injustice. We love beautiful old things *and* make room for new truths.

If you're someone who can honor that, who can cherish both the soft light and the clear truth, then welcome. Welcome, my dear! This is just me. And I am so grateful for your friendship.

Spring

Spring arrives like a gentle awakening:
soft, green shoots pushing through frozen ground,
a reminder that change and hope can coexist.
It's the season of beginning again, of
ideas sprouting, of voices finding their song.
Here we learn to welcome clarity, to let budding
confidence take root, to delight in the
fragile beauty of momentum just beginning.

Fresh with No Mistakes (Yet)

Do you remember that scene
from *Anne of Green Gables*,
where Anne says,

"It is a tremendous consolation
that tomorrow is always fresh
with no mistakes in it."

And Mrs. Stacy replies,
"Well, with no mistakes in it yet."

Each morning,
a fresh start,
a clean slate,
a soft exhale into the new.

But it's also true
that we are human,
wonderfully human
and sometime during the day
we'll stumble.

We'll speak too quickly,
or forget the laundry,
or lose our temper
over something small
and sour.
So when that moment comes,
as it surely will,
can I ask you something, my darling?

Be gentle with yourself.

Pick yourself up,
smooth out your rumpled feelings,
make amends if you need to,
have a laugh if you can,

And carry on.

Forgive yourself,
my dear.

You are doing the very best you can,
and that is
more than enough.

Begin Again Anytime You Like

Spring is the classic time for new beginnings, isn't it? The world smells like rain and freshly turned soil and lilac blossoms. The trees are dressing up in green again, and you can almost hear the daffodils whispering, *It's okay to try again.* Spring practically begs you to begin anew with her fresh mornings and longer days. And little shoots of life poking up through the earth.

Of course, we've always had January 1, with its glittery resolutions and all that New Year, New You business. Some folks feel that hopeful buzz again in September, the start of a school year. Sharpened pencils, new notebooks, sturdy shoes, and the promise of a routine.

But here's something I want you to know, my darling. There are no rules about when you're allowed to begin again. Not one. You don't have to wait for springtime or the turning of the calendar or a Monday morning.

You can start over anytime you like.

You can try again in the middle of a Wednesday afternoon. You can take a breath, let go of yesterday, and gently say to yourself, "Let's give this another go." You can choose to leave the old story behind and begin writing a new chapter, even if the ink from the last one isn't dry yet.

Now let's be honest, you're going to mess up. All of us do. You'll have days when you fall short of your own hopes, when the dishes pile up, the laundry goes sour in the washer, and that one cookie becomes half the bag. That's all right, that's being human. And the beautiful truth is, each new morning brings a new mercy, a new chance.

Every fresh start, even the wobbly ones, carries you a little farther down the road. You don't need a special season to turn toward the light; you just need a quiet moment and a little courage.

And, my dear, you already have both.

The Freedom of Being Yourself

The older I get, the more I understand that it's okay to live a life that others don't understand.

Don't be afraid to be your whole self, my darlings. I've always been a bit of an oddball. As a kid I wore weird glasses. I had braces. I sang way too loudly and way out of tune. I was chubby and really, really, *really* bad at sports.

I was called "weird" to my face more times than I can even count. That used to sting, but somehow not so much anymore. In fact, not at all anymore. I'm not even sure when it happened, but sometime along the way I learned to love that weird little fat girl that I was (and still am, truth be told).

Loving her has helped me discover my true essence. Because here's the thing, my darlings: As long as you're limited by what others find acceptable or appealing, you'll never have enough room to stretch out and become who you're actually meant to be. You'll be too busy checking to see if your edges are showing, too busy adjusting yourself. To avoid being too much, you'll be too busy asking for permission to be exactly what the world needs you to be, your gloriously weird, sparkling, sideways self.

When I was growing up and even in college, being a weirdo wasn't convenient. It wasn't fashionable or cute or empowering or the sort of thing you put on a tote bag. It was just hard.

I didn't fit in. I didn't like the things I was supposed to like. In college, I was maybe a bit too good with the small talk but simultaneously exhausted by those big, loud parties. After about half an hour of the loud music and smoke and hilarious humanity, I just wanted to go find a quiet closet somewhere and have a little lie down all by myself. (I will neither disclose nor deny whether this actually happened more than once.) I was quiet when others were loud, and loud when quiet was expected. I wore vintage slips as loungewear and my dad's 1940s navy bell- bottoms with graphic tees I painted myself. I couldn't do the social choreography that came so easily to others. It all felt like a play I hadn't auditioned for.

I remember thinking, maybe I'll grow out of this. Maybe one day I'll learn how to laugh less often, learn not to care so intensely about every little thing. Learn to dole out my smiles more judiciously and nod thoughtfully in all the appropriate conversational moments. Maybe I'll stop being the girl who got weird looks for reading vintage homemaking guides for entertainment and collecting 1940s hankies.

But surprise! I grew up and I'm still that girl, still weird. Still wearing vintage slips (but not as loungewear anymore!). Still getting excited about the domestic history of mothballs and collecting embroidered tea towels. Still caring too much about things no one else gives a second thought to. Still talking to myself in the produce aisle. Still delighting in strange little things and crying at the fall leaves.

And now I love that about me.

I look at young people now, so bright, so brave, so dazzlingly odd, and I see them do the same dance I once did, the hesitation before speaking their truth. The quiet shrinking, the little edits they make to their expression, their style, their voice. I see them trying to belong without vanishing.

And I want to gently take their hand and whisper, "You don't have to do that."

I hope when they see me—this joyful, chubby, slightly eccentric lady who wears vintage every day and talks to her cats like grandchildren—I hope they feel even the faintest flicker of permission. Permission to be fully themselves. Permission to bloom right where they are, even if it's in the cracks.

Because being different isn't a flaw to fix, it's a thread to follow. A map back to your truest self.

Growing into your full, wild, radiant self is not the backup plan. It's the whole point. And let me tell you the joy that comes from embracing your own weirdness. It's delicious. It's the kind of joy that makes your shoulders drop and your face relax. The kind of joy that makes you hum while dusting and talk to the birds on the windowsill.

So here's to the weirdos. The ones still blooming in the margins. The ones who know too many facts about teacups. The ones who cry over stray cats and make shopping lists from 100-year-old catalogs. The ones who've never quite fit but somehow made a space for themselves anyway.

If that's you, take heart.

You are not broken, you are blooming. You are not too much, you're just enough. You are not lost, you are simply unfolding.

And the world is so much brighter because of your strange sparkling light.

So please, my darling, keep shining exactly as you are.

You are not broken,
you are blooming.
You are not too much,
you're just enough.
You are not lost,
you are simply unfolding.

The Best Decorating Advice I Ever Received

When I was a young woman, I happened to meet a very exclusive, very expensive interior decorator, and she gave me some of the best advice of my life.

I'd asked her some banal question about decorating on a budget or some such thing, and barely restraining her obvious impulse to roll her eyes, she leaned in toward me and whispered conspiratorially, "Ignore the trends. Ignore the rules. Surround yourself with things you love, and eventually they will all work together."

Then she slapped the table and turned away as if to say, "That's that!"

And every year that's passed has only proved her more right. My home is filled with a motley collection of furnishings from all different eras and styles, none of it valuable. Many of the cornerstone pieces are chipped or threadbare or wobbly on one leg.

According to the rules, none of it should work.

But it all does. Because I love it all. And I think that's the rule that matters most.

The Hardest Kind of Self-Care

True confession: I'm a homebody. And not just your average homebody. No, I'm the kind of homebody who could make a sport out of it. An *extreme* sport. Left to my own devices, I can happily watch the weeks slip by without ever stepping past the familiar borders of my own little yard. The grocery store? A nice idea, but they deliver, and delivery is *sooo* much easier. The coffee shop down the street? I have that lovely coffee leftover from breakfast . . . perhaps another time. The world out there spins on, and I'm quite at peace, watching it from my window.

Now, don't misunderstand me, I'm not agoraphobic. My counselor would tell you that too. But she does gently encourage me to nudge myself out into the world every day or two just for my mental health. And I know she's right. The truth is, it's not always easy. Sometimes I go out and, well, I don't enjoy myself. It all feels so crowded, the errands a bit too tedious.

But then there are those other times, the *surprise* times when I come home lighter, brighter, and filled with the kind of quiet joy I didn't expect to find in a simple walk to the park or on a spontaneous coffee date. I find myself surprised by how good the sunshine feels on my skin, how sweet the air smells after a rain, how satisfying it is to chat with that sweet young woman behind the counter at the cafe. Or to run into an old neighbor or to make a new friend.

Every time, no matter how the outing goes, I come home proud because I did the hard thing and I took care of myself.

We've been sold a lovely little picture of self-care, haven't we? The bubble baths, the face masks, the frothy lattes, and manicures. Binge-watching a favorite show while indulging in decadent chocolates. And yes, those things have their time and place. But more and more, I've come to see that real self-care, the kind that nourishes us in the long run, often doesn't feel so cozy in the moment.

Real self-care looks like paying that bill you've been dreading. Making the phone call you've put off for far too long. Washing the dishes instead of letting them soak overnight. Getting up and going for that walk, even when the couch is calling your name. Venturing out of your soft, comfortable bubble and stretching just a bit toward the light, toward the fresh air. Toward life.

Because here's the secret, dear one. The best self-care is the kind that makes life gentler for your future self. It's doing the hard thing today so that tomorrow feels a little easier, a little lighter. And you, you are worth that effort. Every bit of it.

Do One Small Thing

Do you ever look around you and feel that everything has gotten just a little bit out of hand? The house feels messier than you intended. The dishes have somehow multiplied when you weren't looking. You've sat completely still for the whole dang morning. And you can't quite recall the last time you took a proper shower. Oh, my dear one, I know that feeling all too well.

It can feel like you've let things slide for just a bit too long, and now the mountain of things to do feels entirely too steep to climb. It's overwhelming and maybe a little shame-inducing, if we're being completely honest. But before you let that heavy feeling settle in too deeply, I want you to pause. Take a breath. Right now, we're not going to fix everything. We're not going to even try.

Instead, I want you to choose just one small thing. One gentle, doable thing. Wash your favorite mug, the one that makes you smile when you hold it. Wipe off one little surface, a corner of the counter, perhaps. Don't worry about making it perfect; that's not our goal. Our goal is simply movement.

Take it slow, my darling. Rest when you need to. If the thought of a full shower feels too daunting today, that's perfectly fine. Just wash your face, brush your teeth. Run your hands under cool fresh water and feel it ground you. The smallest act of care can bring surprising comfort.

If you have a bit more energy, take a little walk around the block if you can, around your home if that feels better. Even a gentle stretch or a simple flexing of your fingers and toes can remind your body that you are here, you are alive, and you are tending to yourself.

Here's a little secret, my dear one. Those big things that are so scary and overwhelming are nothing more than little things all in a row. Tiny things like a trail of bread crumbs leading you to where you long to be.

So today, do the small things you can do. And tomorrow, do a few more. Be patient with yourself. You're not behind, you're simply on your way.

Potato Week

When all my children were small, there were times when money was tight. I mean *really* tight. We did our best and stretched what we had, but even so, sometimes there just wasn't quite enough. If you've ever been there, you know. Love can fill a home to the rafters, but that doesn't stop worry from slipping in through the cracks.

I remember one spring afternoon in particular, my daughter Millen was performing in the local Special Olympics, and we were all so proud. I packed up the kids, brought our peanut butter sandwiches, and we cheered ourselves hoarse from the sidelines. She was radiant when running, beaming, just shining from the inside out. That part of the day was golden.

But after it was over, we discovered someone had stolen my grocery money right out of my purse. One hundred and seven dollars in a long white envelope, with my grocery list written on one side and my meal plan on the other. Every cent I'd set aside for food that week—gone. I remember sitting in the parking lot, stunned. All I had left was $35 in vouchers for the farmers' market, some kind of promotion from the county agricultural committee. It didn't seem like enough.

But the next morning, we went to the farmers' market. I told myself we needed to buy the biggest volume of food we could manage. And there they were, beautiful russet potatoes piled high in dusty burlap sacks. I bought 50 pounds of them with my vouchers. It felt like a gamble, but it was all I could think to do.

That week, we had potatoes in every form you can imagine. Baked, boiled, mashed, crisped in the skillet with onions. We made a game of never eating them prepared the same way twice. One night I grated them into pancakes, and we ate them with applesauce from the back of the pantry. Another night I sliced them thin, layered them with some leftover shreds of cheese and called it a casserole. The kids loved it.

And you know what? Those potatoes were the most delicious I'd ever tasted. Maybe it was the hunger, or the memory of the sunshine at the market, or the joy of recalling Millen running her races that golden day, or the relief when my silly and brave little potato gamble paid off. I know part of it was the pride I felt in feeding my children when it felt like I might not be able to. Maybe it was all of it together. Whatever it was, that week has become a legend in our family. Even now years later, my grown children will say, "Remember potato week?" and we all smile. We marvel at how delicious those potatoes were and laugh at all the crazy potato dishes we came up with. We didn't feel poor that week, we felt lucky. So lucky. So blessed and safe.

Darling, sometimes life throws a twist in the road that you couldn't have imagined or prepared for. Sometimes someone will take something from you that you need. That you desperately need. It's not fair. It's not easy, but somehow you make do. You gather what you can, you feed who you love, and you get through. Somehow that dusty bag of potatoes bought in a week when we didn't have much turned out to be so much more than enough. It became comfort and nourishment, laughter and memory.

Caring for Self, Caring for Community

I sometimes feel fragile, vulnerable, like I'm grieving something I can't quite put into words. On those days, I might retreat a little. Indulge in things that aren't especially good for me. Or, just as often, I swing the other way and punish myself by overworking, denying myself rest or softness, as if that will prove I'm still strong.

But I'm learning. Slowly, softly, I'm learning that balance doesn't come easily, but it does come. It turns out balance isn't always something I can create myself. I find it most often in the spaces where my life brushes up against others: when I share a word, or when I let myself be held by the kindness of strangers-turned-friends.

I can tell from the kind and sometimes aching comments left in my social media feed that so many people are carrying grief of their own. Private pain. Weariness. Silent battles. I always try to respond to those comments with tenderness and encouragement. But sometimes I miss one. Or I don't get to it right away. And that breaks my heart, truly. I never want someone to feel unseen.

But then, something beautiful happens. I notice others—people like you, dear reader—stepping in. Responding with kindness, empathy, hope. And when I see that, I think, *These are my people.* This is the kind of world I want to dwell in. One where kindness multiplies. Where vulnerability is met with warmth, not judgment.

If you're feeling bruised or weary today, know this: You're not alone. I've been there. I still go there sometimes. But I've learned that fragility is not a failing. It's a signal. A call to softness, to care, to community.

When the world feels like too much, let's be a soft place to land for each other. And when you're ready, I'll be right here—hand extended, heart open. Let's walk this path together.

A Visit to the White House

Not long ago, this old lady, who leads a very small, rather quiet life, received an invitation to a reception at the White House to meet President Joseph Robinette Biden at a reception for Women's History Month. Can you imagine? My first instinct was to decline. It all felt too big, too far, too out of place in my gentle little world. I imagined a room full of important, accomplished people in heels and sleek designer dresses, and then *me.* Roly-poly me in a vintage frock with matching gloves and hat.

But I went. Not alone, mind you. I had help. Encouragement. Loving hands who helped with travel arrangements, who talked me through my nerves, who made sure the practicalities were covered: budget, childcare, my intense dislike of airports, to name a few. My people made the big thing smaller. Made it doable.

And so I went. I visited the White House. I saw the president. And he was lovely. I shook hands, took pictures, stood in awe of the history and the chandeliers. And I remembered that even quiet lives can have grand moments.

A Little Bedroom Revival

I sometimes let my bedroom fall into an abominable state. Not my daughter's bedroom. Millen's room is always pristine, tidied daily with fresh lavender-scented linens without fail every Monday. Never my kitchen, where the sink is scalded and countertops disinfected every evening, and sparkling-clean day-of-the-week dishtowels appear each morning. Living room, dining room, front hall . . . Well, there might be a bit of dust and the occasional pile of mail (or other types of the detritus of life), but generally these spaces are clean and tidy and welcoming too. But my bedroom? I'm almost embarrassed to tell you! The windowsill is battered from weather and time, and one of the cats, dear Caoimhe—little cranky, little odd, little Caoimhe—has taken to shredding the curtain. Everything in my bedroom can get a bit untidy, a little dusty and, truth be told, more than a little neglected.

When this happens, there is no use fussing. I best just get to work!

My Nana taught me to clean from the top down, so I begin there, dusting the corners of the ceiling. Gently brushing away the cobwebs that no doubt thought they had squatter's rights. Then off come the linens. The bed is stripped bare. Off come the doilies and the dresser scarves, the old tissue box cover that's lost its shape, and all the little odds and ends tucked here and there.

Today I'm even doing the curtains. They'll be washed, line-dried, starched, and pressed. The one torn by Caoimhe will need a little mending. I'll sit with that in the evening, needle and thread in hand, and repair it the old-fashioned way.

I take a basket and gather everything that belongs elsewhere: hair clips, socks gone astray, a mug or two. The wastebasket gets a thorough sorting as well. During one memorable deep clean, I even found my favorite pin, a simple Black Lives Matter button I had worn through a rainstorm once. The black dye in the printed background bled into the white letters, softening them into sepia shadows. The background has faded in patches, worn with time and weather. It doesn't look new anymore, and I like it that way. Later, I'll ask my son Noah to help me with repairing the finish on the windowsill, but for now, I give it a good scrub and wipe down the baseboards while I'm at it. A quick sweep with the dust mop and the floor is already shining a smile back at me for my attention.

There's nothing in the world quite like the scent of freshly laundered bed linens. I use a splash of lavender water in the final rinse of the washing machine. It lingers on the pillowcases and makes me feel just the tiniest bit spoiled, safe, and cared for.

Next I attend to the furniture, offering it a gentle rubdown with beeswax polish, which is still my favorite. It brings the old wood back to life. Once the dresser scarves are clean and crisp, they go right back in their places. I beat the dust out of the rug and give it a good brushing. While mending that curtain takes the better part of an hour, I don't mind one bit. It feels nice to sit and stitch for a while.

I dust every knickknack, place everything just so, and pick out a soft nightgown for later—one of my favorites, pressed with lavender water and lay over the foot of the bed like a promise.

I spend the whole day deep-cleaning my bedroom, and by the end of it, I am tired, even a bit sore. But oh, the joy! The deep kind of joy that comes not from perfection but from care.

Isn't it funny how we care so well for others but often forget to care for ourselves?

Be Your Whole Wonderful, Glorious Self

You have a choice.

You can spend your life worrying about what others think. Folding yourself up into a tidier, more acceptable shape, quieting your shine so no one mistakes it for arrogance. You can tuck in your joy so it doesn't take up too much space. You can stay small. You can stay quiet. You can keep trying to win the approval of people who will never be satisfied. But here's the truth, my dears: No matter what you do, there will always be someone ready to find fault. There will always be critics. There will always be cruel people, and yes, even the well-meaning ones: the family members, the neighbors, the old friends who think they know how you should live your life better than you do.

There will always be people who misunderstand you, who disapprove, who think your dreams are silly or your clothes too outlandish or your personality too much. But you have a choice, my dear one. A very important one.

You don't have to give those people power.

You don't have to let their disapproval become your direction. Their fear doesn't have to become your cage. Their opinion doesn't get to shape your joy.

Now, maybe you're not quite there yet. Maybe you can't just let the criticism roll off your back, at least not all the time. That's okay. Here's what you can do: Find a little corner of your life and make it yours. Some tiny place where you can assert your individuality. A drawer full of glittery socks. A bookshelf filled with the toys you secretly wanted as a child and never got. A music playlist you never share with anyone. A lipstick shade that gives you a zing of joy when you catch sight of yourself in the rearview mirror.

Let that one small place be a start.

I've always loved vintage clothing, especially from the 1930s and 1940s—the late 1940s in particular. I've collected so many beautiful pieces over the years, and while I wore some of them, they were always just an accent. A subtle nod to the past added on to a more conventional outfit. I tucked soft peach pointelle camisoles beneath my ubiquitous middle-aged lady tunic tops. I wore rayon stockings under jeans and sneakers. I didn't want to look too outlandish. Or too costumed. So I softened it all, toned it down, tried not to draw too much attention.

But one morning in 2020, in the thickest fog of the pandemic, locked down, isolated, unsure of so much, I stood in front of my closet and realized something. I could wear whatever the heck I wanted. No one would be seeing me. No one was coming over. I wasn't going anywhere. There was no one to judge me.

And so I did it.

I dressed exactly as I pleased, full vintage from the skin out. A boned corselet, rayon undies, a soft cotton housedress, sturdy little oxfords, and a cashmere sweater draped over my shoulders.

It was quiet, it was ordinary, and it was absolutely glorious.

I felt so myself.

I simply chose joy, and I wore it.

And that, my darling, is the whole point.

Fight for your joy.

Fight for it fiercely. And when you find it, hold on with both hands. Don't loosen your grip just because someone else doesn't understand it. Don't lose your vibrancy simply because someone else doesn't see the value.

Wear what you want, say what you mean. Live your life in full, vibrant color.

Be unconventional if that's who you are. Be soft, be bold, be complicated, be strange. Be your whole wonderful, glorious self.

Because you know what?

The world needs you. Not a quieter version of you. Not a tidier, more palatable version. You, exactly as you are.

You are not too much to handle or too little to notice. You are not the wrong shape or the wrong story. You are needed. *You*.

So go ahead and live. Wear the vintage clothes . . . or the glittery socks! Laugh loudly. Say no when you mean no. Say yes when you mean yes.

And never let someone else's discomfort rob you of your light. Your joy is worth protecting.

Your truth is worth honoring. And your life is worth living . . . fully, freely, gloriously. Exactly as you are.

The world needs you. Not a quieter version of you. Not a tidier, more palatable version. You, exactly as you are.

The Cats on My Porch

People often assume I've always been a passionate cat lover. And I suppose, by now, I am. But it didn't begin that way. I like to say I'm not so much a cat lover as I am a suffering-hater. And oh, how feral cats do suffer.

They shiver through winters and swelter in the summer heat. They fall ill, get injured, and receive no care. They starve. Their wounds go untreated, their pain unnoticed. And the kittens— malnourished, sick, their eyes crusted shut—well, they just about break your heart.

Years ago, I could barely afford vet care and food for the single pet cat we had. But I couldn't bear the suffering I saw in the strays on my street. So somehow, I made a way. A little at a time, I started feeding them. I couldn't get them fixed or vaccinated at first, but I reached out to rescue groups and asked for help. And, bless those kind-hearted rescuers, they took me under their wing. They mentored me, trained me. Taught me how to trap the wildest tomcats, how to recognize signs of illness, how to soothe a frightened mother with her litter in tow.

With their help, I slowly learned the rhythms of this quiet, persistent work. I learned that some cats can be tamed and go on to become beloved companions in someone else's home. And some will never want that. Some choose the wild life. And it matters to me to honor that choice.

So I care for them.

My porch has become a haven. When it's hot outside, there are bowls of cool, clean water and little fountains that bubble just enough to keep things fresh. There's food every morning and every evening. Supplements for the aging cats, extra treats for growing kittens. In winter, there are heated shelters packed with straw. In summer, shade and cooling mats. I tend to them as best I can, and when they're sick or injured, I take them to the vet.

Indoors, my own pet cats live lives of leisure. They are brushed and played with and generally adored. They lounge on sunny windowsills and supervise the baking from atop the kitchen chairs. Their lives are gentle. Safe. Loved.

But the wild ones on my porch, who will never curl up in anyone's lap, are just as deserving of safety, health, joy. And I will do whatever I can to make that happen. Not just to alleviate their suffering but to give them a life worth living.

Maybe that's what I've come to love most of all—not just the cats themselves but the opportunity to say, in the smallest, kindest ways: Your life matters. You matter.

Even if you never come inside.

Sometimes the Hardest One to Be Kind to Is Yourself

My friend Chris and I were talking once about the pressure to always be productive, how our sense of worth gets tangled up in the things we accomplish. The lists we check off. The goals we reach. He asked me, "How do you get past that, though? How do you move on?" And in that moment, grasping for an answer, I mumbled something vague and overly simple about loving yourself.

I owe him a better answer.

Because learning to love yourself isn't simple. It's not a switch you flip. It's not a slogan you chant three times a day in the mirror. It's a practice. A long, gentle, faltering practice.

If I could go back to that conversation, I would say this: You have to teach yourself to value yourself. Even when you don't feel valuable. Especially when you don't. You have to act as if you are someone worth caring for. You have to make a habit of treating yourself like someone precious.

Feed yourself kindly. Speak to yourself gently. Clothe yourself warmly. Surround yourself with beauty and softness, even in small ways. Let yourself rest.

When it feels hard to do that, picture little you. Tiny child you, with messy hair and grubby fingers. Teenager you, trying so hard to be good and grown-up and lovable. Remember what

Feed yourself kindly.
Speak to yourself gently.
Clothe yourself warmly.
Surround yourself
with beauty and softness,
even in small ways.
Let yourself rest.

it felt like to be smaller and more tender, how easily bruised your spirit could be.

And then, my darling, treat yourself today like you needed to be treated back then. Because you are still that same person. The same heart lives inside you. You are every bit as lovable now as you were when you were tiny. You are every bit as bold and gorgeous as teenage you. You don't have to earn gentleness. You don't have to prove your right to rest. You are not a project to improve or a puzzle to solve. You are a human being, growing, healing, unfolding. And you are so precious.

You always have been.

Do More of What Makes You Happy

What makes you happy, my dear?

I wonder about that sometimes. We get so busy, so tangled in the lists and shoulds and waiting- for-laters that we forget to ask ourselves what actually brings us joy. The small kind of joy: the kind you can hold in your hands, tuck in the pocket of your heart, and save for later.

For me, happiness looks like setting my hair, brushing it out slowly, curling it just right. There's something about getting that front curl to fall just so that feels both grounding and a little bit magical. It's not about looking perfect. It's about the ritual, the rhythm of care, the gentle way of telling myself that I matter.

And then, of course, there's coffee. A warm cup in my favorite mug, steam rising like a soft breeze. I'll stir in a touch of maple syrup, maybe reach for a little cookie if I have one. Not because I need a treat to distract or numb me but because I want to enjoy the moment fully with no rushing past it. Just me and the quiet sweetness of being alive.

But that's me. What about you? What makes you happy?

Is it a walk outside in the fresh air, where the sky stretches wide and the wind lifts your hair from your shoulders? Is it the beauty in a loved one's face, something you catch when they're not looking, when they are simply being themselves? Is it the deep laughter that comes from a rollicking time with lots and lots of friends, where everything feels a little too loud in the best way? Or is it dancing or maybe baking? Maybe being completely alone in peaceful quiet, where you can hear your own heart again.

Whatever it is that brings you joy, my darling, do *that.* If it doesn't hurt anyone else, make space for it.

Let it happen more. Those small, ordinary joys matter more than we think. They're not distractions, they're reminders. They're lifelines.

So take the walk. Pour the coffee. Set your hair. Play the music. Sit in silence. Laugh too loudly. Do more of the things that make you happy.

You don't need a reason, you only need the moment.

The Gift of Rest

Recently, I took a week off to rest and recover after a medical procedure, but in the back of my mind, I thought I'd still manage to do a bit of filming, some editing, a little writing, perhaps even some housecleaning or sewing. Instead, I rested. That's it. I rested and recovered.

I was going to apologize for it. I was going to say sorry for being lazy, but then I caught myself. I remembered that week I was doing the best I could, and right now, as I'm recalling those days of rest, I'm choosing kindness.

I had to laugh at myself when I set out to tidy my dining room and had to stop after only a few minutes to rest. That entire day was spent just resting, and the next morning my dining room table still had no tablecloth. But that's okay. Rest matters. Grace matters when we don't live up to our own expectations. It's an act of love to meet ourselves with gentleness instead of blame.

Some days I rest all day long, and some days that's the best thing I can do. It can be so hard to slow down. Maybe you're ill or worn thin or brokenhearted. Maybe you're just tired. Yet still we push ourselves. There are responsibilities. People might be counting on you. And yes, when we stop to rest, there may be others who don't understand, people who frown upon or question or disapprove of your choices. But their misunderstanding does not make your need for rest

Rest is not laziness,
it's strength in disguise.
It's how we restore
ourselves so that we can
rise again with joy.

any less real. So please, take the time you need. Give your beautiful body what it needs.

Rest is not laziness, it's strength in disguise. It's how we restore ourselves so that we can rise again with joy.

During the long, strange years of the pandemic, I caught COVID, and it hit me hard. My recovery was slow, full of false starts and frustrating setbacks. I'd feel a little better and throw myself back into normal life, only to relapse and need more rest. I hated asking for help. I wanted to be the helper, not the helped.

But I needed help, and help came.

There were friends who stayed with me and friends who left me sweetly alone, who sensed when silence was the greater kindness. There were online friends, perhaps folks just like you, who told me to take all the time I needed. I can't tell you how much that meant to me.

Accepting help can be hard, but giving help and receiving it are both holy acts. When we receive help with grace, we offer the giver something sacred in return. Trust, vulnerability, the chance to love, the chance to show our love.

And when I'm feeling scattered or discombobulated, after a rough stretch, be it from a migraine or the happy chaos of a houseguest, I try to begin again. I reach for order. I make new lists. I reset my routines. I take comfort in prioritizing the small good things: my health, my peace, my rhythm.

Because healing takes time. Because fresh starts are always available. Because rest is not a luxury. It's a kindness—one we all deserve.

Little Signs You're Growing into Yourself

You don't always realize it at first. Growing into yourself is quiet work. Gentle work. It doesn't always come with big breakthroughs or loud revelations. Mostly you probably won't even notice you're making progress. Sometimes it looks like tiny changes that feel too small to matter.

But they do matter. Oh, they do.

So here, my darling, are just a few small signs that you're growing into your truest self:

- You laugh without second-guessing yourself.
- You wear what makes you smile, even if no one else gets it.
- You find yourself saying no without apology.
- You say yes with delight.
- You realize you'd rather be kind than cool, kind than clever, or even right. And sometimes, that kindness includes being kind to yourself.
- You stop chasing flawless. You don't even jog toward it anymore.
- You find beauty in places you used to overlook.
- You decorate with things that younger you longed for.

- You talk to the birds. And the teapot. And occasionally the vacuum.
- You lose the need to explain yourself. And gain more peace in just being.
- You rediscover old hobbies that made you weird as a kid and now make you joyful as an adult.
- You look in the mirror and think, *There you are. Hello, my darling*!

Growing into yourself isn't about becoming someone else. It's about returning to the you that you always were. A little wiser. A little softer. A lot more sparkly.

And if you're not quite there yet, that's okay too. You're on your way. And oh, what a lovely way it is.

Summer

Summer is the season of fullness, of fruit heavy on the vine and hearts unafraid to shine. Days stretch long, encouraging boldness and bloom. There's a confidence that rises with the heat, a radiant sense that maybe—just maybe—we've found our stride. In these bright essays, we'll rest in the warmth of momentum, celebrating beauty in its most exuberant form.

Born Worthy

I've always loved beautiful things,
And I've loved working
To make the things around me
As lovely as I could

Still—
There have been times
When I felt guilty
About wasting time
On such frivolities.

But the longer I've lived,
The more certain I have become in this:

No bit of beauty is ever wasted.

Even if it's just for your own family,
Even if it's just for yourself

My darlings,
I hope today
That you're surrounded by beautiful things—

Because, my friend,
You were meant for beauty.

Gentle Rebellion

For most of my life, no one else I knew shared my peculiar passions. I was enchanted by old, out-of-date housewares and linens, supposedly frumpy clothing, and gentle, unhurried ways of living. I moved through the world slowly and needed more time than most to finish what others seemed to breeze through. I am dozy and day-dreamy. I was drawn to things others overlooked and bored by things they found exciting. Where they craved novelty, I craved familiarity. Where they rushed forward, I lingered.

In childhood, I was "a joy to have in class" but also "lacking in diligence and focus." In young adulthood, I often felt isolated, even when surrounded by friends who loved me. In motherhood, I struggled to keep up with the pace everyone else seemed to be managing just fine. But with each season of life, I grew more comfortable in my own skin and more certain that the way I moved through the world—slowly, strangely, sweetly—was not only acceptable but right. For me.

Over time, I discovered that if I simply stayed the course, if I let my own light shine instead of hiding it or dimming it, others would find me. Kindred spirits appeared, one by one, like stars winking in the night sky. Sometimes we only shared a brief moment, a glimmer of connection. Other times, they became lifelong companions. But always, I was reminded:

the world is full of others who are also quietly different, also walking softly on their own unusual paths.

Not everything that's important to others will matter to you. And not everything that matters deeply to you will make sense to others. That's okay. Our joy has value even when no one else understands it. The piles of books you collect or antique cars or the very latest style of new shoes! The way you hum while you bake, your passion for mountain hikes, your quest to create that perfect pot of chili, or your collection of odd buttons. These pursuits aren't frivolous. They're *your* joy. And joy is never frivolous.

Allow yourself, my darling, to be unconventional. To like what you like, even if no one else does. To live in a way that feels beautiful and right and true. There's a quiet power in that. When you live joyfully and authentically, you give others permission to do the same. And some of them, people you may never meet, will watch you from afar and think, *If she can be herself so beautifully, maybe I can too.*

Nurture that ember of joy. Feed it with the things that make your heart sing. Even if they're small. Especially if they're small.

Recently, I received a letter asking if I had any advice for living a happy and fulfilling life. I'm not sure I have advice, exactly. But I can tell you that accepting my own uniqueness, my "weirdness," as the girls in my junior high gym class so graciously called it, was the beginning of everything for me. When I began to let go of the things that never truly mattered to me—success, popularity, fitting in—and began instead to build a life around the things that did, that's when I found peace. Beauty. Joy.

These days, I've traded ambition for contentment, speed for stillness, applause for quiet connection. I've built a life that wouldn't suit many people, and that's the whole point. It suits me.

Don't be afraid to be different, my dear. Let the world see your whole wonderful, weird self. You never know who might fall in love with that exact version of you. You never know what friends you might make or whose lives you might quietly change.

Dare to be unconventional. Dare to be joyful. Dare to be you.

Beauty Is Always Right Around the Corner

It was such a dreary, dripping morning. My normally bright and cheerful front porch felt gloomy and dark. The old wicker furniture was damp and creaking. The cushions and linens that looked sparkling clean in bright sunlight somehow looked gray. My favorite grumpy little stray cat was even grumpier than usual. Her black-and-white-patterned fur looked soaked through, raindrops clinging to the ends of her absurdly long whiskers. She lifted first one paw and then the other, as if trying to find respite from contact with the sodden front steps.

I didn't want to set foot on the driveway where I walk laps each morning, but I resolutely set out anyway. The cement sidewalk was wet, and it drenched my slippers almost immediately. I regretted not changing into my sneakers. Raindrops dripped slowly down the side panels of my youngest son Noah's glorious old 1951 Hudson Esmeralda and pooled in the curves on her hood. As I squeezed through the narrow passage between the car and the tall garden on the side of the driveway, my robe soaked up the water. Every lap I walked, my robe absorbed more and more liquid until I was drenched through. My eyes were down, focused on my muddy feet. But as I grimly turned around the final corner of my final lap, I looked up, and my eye caught a flash of the brightest red and orange, and vivid green. There, tucked between the trash cans and the gate to the back garden, was a little forgotten planter tumbling with little bright zinnias on tall green stems. The blooms bobbed as the rain dribbled down, and they curtsied to me as I passed by. I smiled. And I remembered, beauty is always right around the corner if you're looking for it.

When my children were young, I worked long hours, and there wasn't much money to spare, but together we cherished the beauty wherever we found it. I collected mismatched embroidered napkins from the thrift store, and we saved pretty little postcards in a special box. I splurged on a wooden stand from the Waldorf supply shop, and every morning the kids and I would make a ceremony of choosing just the right picture postcard to place in it. We'd light a candle, and we'd take the time to drink in the loveliness. It was a favorite time of our days and, oh, how we enjoyed those moments!

In the summer evenings, right around the time of our late-summer sunsets, I spend a few minutes scurrying around on my front porch. I fill my watering cans so they're all ready and waiting for the morning when I water all my flowerpots. Some folks think it's a lot of extra work just to fill my porch with flowers, but it's worth it to me.

I put out nutritious food and fresh flowing water for the neighborhood stray cats. I cover all the vintage fabrics on my porch furniture with sturdy, washable coverings to protect them from muddy little kitty feet overnight. I put out soft little beds so the cats will be comfy, even if they can't nestle themselves in the cushions as they'd prefer. Some folks think it's rather silly of me to welcome stray cats in the same space where I use fragile textiles, and maybe they're right. Probably

I am a bit silly. It takes a bit of extra work for me to keep my old things safe and my sweet kitty friends comfy, but that's okay. It's worth it to me to have the pleasure of them both.

Do the things that matter to you, my dear, even if they don't make sense to any other person. Do the things that make you happy.

Every Faded Stitch

One of my favorite things to do in this world is laundering my vintage linens. These little odds and ends give me such joy every day. And part of that joy is the gentle care they require. I use special detergents. I pretreat the stains, soak them for hours, and rinse them in many changes of water. Then I hang them out to dry in the clean, bright sunlight and let the breeze finish the job. The whole process feels like an offering, a loving gift to myself—their beauty a gift I offer to those I welcome into my home.

Most of these pieces are a good deal older than I am. Some are in pristine condition, and I do my best to keep them that way. But more of them have flaws, worn spots, broken threads, the kind of translucence that comes only with time. Some of their stains will never come out no matter what I do. But I don't mind. Sometimes I think I love the imperfect ones best of all. Sometimes I think their flaws make them even more beautiful.

There's an old Mr. Rogers song called "Please Don't Think It's Funny" that I think of when I'm caring for old, beautiful things. It's about a teddy bear. "He's old, but he's still strong." Isn't that lovely? There's strength and softness in wear, in things that have endured.

Many of the things that are most precious to me would be worthless to someone else. Old embroidered tablecloths, threadbare and tea-stained. Dresses I've worn and loved almost to tatters. I see the patches, the unraveling lace, the dark spots, and I see the artistry in every faded stitch. I think of the beloved ones who gave them to me. I remember the dinners and the heartbreaks and the laughter in rooms graced by them. The way this little apron hem flounced as my child danced with me once long ago. The way that napkin felt in my lap at a table full of family and friends chattering away, lively and warm.

It can be tempting to want everything fresh and new, shiny, bright, and utterly unworn. Everything matching and the latest style, easy-care fabrics and wipe-clean everything. There is a weight to aged things, heavy with memories, and yes, a few stains as well! Those 70-year-old linens will rarely be featured in a trendy home-decorating magazine. The dresses I made from ancient feed sack fabric will never be the latest style. But the latest style will never fit me quite like that dress that has molded itself to my figure over years of wear. Those decidedly not-trendy sheets are far softer than anything new. The way the morning sunlight shines through my patched and mended curtains can't be reproduced by anything that hasn't existed for years.

And perhaps that's the quiet gift of old things: Every year they endure, they prove their strength. Their very weight becomes a kind of testimony, a heaviness that isn't burden but ballast. They remind us that beauty is not always fragile, that usefulness and grace can last a lifetime, or even longer.

Everyday Magic

Sometimes life can feel magical.

If we're very lucky, when we're little, we have adults around us who delight in adding magic to our days. A surprise trip for ice cream. A glittering garland hung just because, a bubble bath by candlelight. They remind us that the world is not only safe but special. This magic teaches us that we are special.

But once we're grown, life can begin to feel dry, responsible, predictable, very *non*-magical.

Guess what, my dear one: you can create your own magic.

Take the pretty route to work, even if it takes a few minutes longer. Buy your favorite snacks— not the practical ones but the ones that make you smile just to see them in the cupboard. Decorate for the seasons and go all out. It doesn't have to cost much. A few cheerful pumpkins, some fairy lights, or even a basket of old toys from your childhood can change the entire mood of your home.

Appreciate the lovely chaos of a full room, laughter echoing. Then relish the quiet when it's just you and your thoughts. Make rituals out of ordinary things: your morning coffee, lighting a candle at twilight, that special hand lotion you put on last thing before turning out the lights at night.

We have more power over our mood than we're often told. And just think, my darling, that bright orange pumpkin on your kitchen counter? It can bring you real joy. That silly little snack tucked away in the cupboard? A tiny treasure.

We're often led to believe that the good life is a grand, polished thing, always out of reach, so sophisticated, so expensive! Always requiring more. But that idea? It's a myth.

A happy life is made up of small, beautiful things, all in a row. And that kind of life is within your reach.

Maybe you're the one now making magic for someone else, a little sparkler of a human who delights in the magic you create. Or maybe, just maybe, no one ever made magical moments for sparkling little you. And if that's the case, I want you to know something very important: It's not too late.

You can still have the magic. You can still be wrapped in warmth, still be delighted by sparkle and spice, because magic doesn't end when we become responsible adults. It just shifts.

A happy life is made up of small, beautiful things, all in a row. And that kind of life is within your reach.

Reality Is Sweeter Than the Vision

Vinti and I are unlikely friends, to be sure. He lives with his wonderful boyfriend in a bustling German city: theaters, lecture halls, and traffic jams just a few steps out from his flat, vintage events, and ancient castles just a short drive away. I live with my daughter in a quiet American village, where the flower lady at the grocery store knows all my children's names and the fireflies come out in early June. He dresses in a carefully curated Edwardian style, while I prefer my comfortable 1940s housedresses and a freshly pinned curl. He speaks flawless English while I can't even properly pronounce *guten Tag*. But in spite of the distance, the differences, and the many small peculiarities that make us who we are, we recognize something familiar in each other. A shared affection for beauty and detail, a love of the aesthetic past, tempered always by a thoughtful understanding of the injustices and hardships it held. We both live with one foot in the present and the other gently dipped into the past.

I'm not sure exactly when Vinti and I first got acquainted. I suppose it started, as these things often do nowadays, by commenting on each other's videos. A few friendly exchanges led to a string of messages. One evening he surprised me with a video call. I sent him a list of books by an old favorite author. We talked about vintage fashion, about history, about the quiet oddness of being ourselves. And then suddenly, naturally, like the way hot tea steams into the air, we were friends.

And truly, Vinti has never once given me a bad piece of advice. I'm not sure why he likes me so much, but he laughs at my jokes more often than not, and that might just be part of the charm.

In September 2023, Vinti planned a visit to the United States—to my very own state, in fact—and neither of us could resist the chance to spend time together in person. I invited him to my home, my little cottage in my little village. When I thought ahead to Vinti's visit, I had all sorts of plans. I pictured long, leisurely sit-and-stare mornings with steaming mugs (coffee for me, tea for him) on my front porch. I thought we'd bake together, maybe arrange flowers, sift through my box of vintage patterns. I imagined we'd sew him a pair of slippers or even a shirt. And oh, the content we'd create! Two old pals with our phone cameras in search of good lighting. I could see it all so clearly.

But none of that happened. Instead, we walked, we talked, we laughed, we made little messes and solved big problems. We created new memories and completely forgot to turn on the camera. The videos we had envisioned drifted aside like petals in the wind, and we didn't mind a bit. Vinti helped me and my youngest son, Noah, string fairy lights across the porch ceiling. That evening we sat out there for hours under the glow of those tiny lights, talking about life, loss, dreams, and everything in between.

We visited a nearby living history museum. My dear daughter Millen, who took to him instantly, insisted on holding his hand the entire way home, and Vinti, true to form, held hers right back, with the openhearted affection he offers so freely. He met my friends. He was folded into our lives with ease. He became not just a visitor but a beloved part of our little community. He is so loved here.

The visit did not follow the plan I had in my mind, but oh, my gracious, how wonderful it was! So much better than I ever could have planned. It was not the visit I'd pictured, but it was so much more real, more nourishing, more beautiful.

And here's the bit of advice I give you, my darling: Let the moment be what it is. Hold your plans loosely like water in your hands. Let them spill and puddle if they must, because sometimes what replaces them is even more glorious than you can imagine.

Sometimes the best gift you can give yourself and the people you love is space. Space for joy to surprise you. Space for connection to unfold naturally without expectation or performance. Space to be fully present with the luminous, imperfect, glorious people in your life.

It's tempting to clutch tightly to our schedules and our ideas. To want the moment to live up to the daydream. But sometimes reality outshines even the sweetest dream. Sometimes the best content is never captured. The most meaningful memories are never posted. Sometimes the most magical part of life happens when no one is looking.

I'm so grateful I was paying attention.

Sometimes the best gift
you can give yourself and the
people you love is space.
Space for joy to surprise you.
Space for connection to
unfold naturally without
expectation or performance.
Space to be fully present
with the luminous, imperfect,
glorious people in your life.

Overflow

Once, while placing an online grocery order, I accidentally ordered twice the amount of flowers I intended. Totally my fault, and concerningly, I already had plenty of blooms left from the week before.

At first, I panicked a little. Then came the guilt. How extravagant! How unnecessary. But as I stood in my kitchen surrounded by all those flowers, I thought back to the years when a single bloom felt like a luxury. I'd splurge on one precious flower, place it in a vase in the center of the dining room table, and the children and I would stretch out every ounce of beauty from that solitary stem.

But that day, I had abundance. And oh, what a glorious thing that is. Pale pink roses clustered in a piece of vintage pottery on my mantelpiece. Bright red tulips standing cheerfully on my gingham kitchen counter. A grand, glorious mess of mixed blooms overflowing from a heavy, old vase on the pine dining room server. And then a tiny vase no bigger than a salt shaker, cradling the sweet little flowers with stems too short for any other vessel. The house was blooming, quite literally, and so was my spirit.

Abundance is a funny thing, isn't it?

My daughter Millen doesn't care much for flowers, but give her a solid morning workout with a pep talk from her beloved JD Roberto streamed onto her laptop at precisely 9 A.M. every morning, followed by an afternoon of dancing and singing along with the Wiggles, and her cup runneth over. My son Noah finds his abundance in travel: an adventure, a suitcase half-packed, and a train to catch.

And me? These days my life feels as though it's spilling over with joy-giving things—small, silly, and sacred. And I'm so grateful.

But maybe the most beautiful part of abundance is this: the freedom to share it. That week of the preponderance of flowers, I filled a mason jar with the prettiest blooms, and I took them to the sweet neighbor on my left. I filled another jar, just as lovely, and took it to the rather difficult neighbors on my right. Because kindness doesn't always need to be easy to be worth it. I wrapped a handful of cheerful daisies in a vintage hanky and surprised a friend when we met for coffee. Each time I gave some of my bounty away, the abundance grew.

What silly little thing fills your heart with joy? What unexpected everyday treasure floods your soul with contentment?

I wish you beauty, whatever that looks like for you. I wish you comfort, however it arrives. I wish you so much abundance that you can't help but give some of it away.

I wish you a life that blooms.

The Joy Drawer

I have a junk drawer. Well, truth be told, I have about half a dozen junk drawers in various parts of my house. In the upstairs bathroom, in the kitchen, in the unused nightstand on the opposite side of my bed. The other day, as I was cleaning out my sewing room junk drawer, I had a thought. Now my darlings, hear me out . . . I've been thinking lately about keeping a joy drawer. Not a metaphorical one, though I do love a good metaphor: a literal drawer. I'm thinking that the almost empty one in my old pine server will do just fine. The one next to the silverware, right below that wide drawer with all the freshly pressed napkins. A real, actual wooden drawer I can open when the day feels heavy and gray, or when the weight of my own impossibly unrealistic expectations weighs me down.

Maybe I'll fill it with old love notes from my children or postcards from friends. A tiny seashell. A piece of ribbon. A candle that smells like that morning we had the best blueberry pancakes ever. Maybe a button from my grandmother's old blue tweed coat. Maybe it's a peppermint, or a fortune from a cookie that made the whole table laugh out loud.

The point is not usefulness. The point is gladness.

I suppose we all need somewhere to keep our joy. Someplace that says yes, that moment mattered. That bright little moment belonged to me. Some people write them down, some take pictures, some hum the tune that was playing on that beautiful golden day, back when everything was okay, even if just for a second.

Joy is sneaky that way. She tiptoes in on quiet feet. She smiles oh-so kindly at us. She lifts her eyebrows as if to say, "Let me in, my dear one. Laugh with me!" She leaves lovely little traces of herself behind. And it's our job, my darling, to catch her in the act, to let her in, to laugh with her . . . or maybe just smile if that's the best we can do. To collect all the little bits she has left behind and store them up somewhere safe and sound so we can return to them when we need them most.

After all, a joy drawer isn't just a place to store things.

It's a place to remember who you are and to revisit what lights you up.

7 Out of 10

I used to believe that if I just worked hard enough, tried earnestly enough, or planned things just right, I could make everything turn out just the way I wanted. I thought if I was kind enough, people would never misunderstand me. If I cleaned well enough, the house would finally stay clean. If I loved hard enough, no one would ever leave. I thought I could get it all.

But, my darling, the truth I've come to sit gently with is this: most of life at its best is about 7 out of 10 of what we'd hoped.

Now I know that might sound sad at first, but I promise it's not because 7 out of 10 is plenty. And here's the important part: It's not that every single day is just seven-tenths wonderful. Some days will surprise you with a perfect 10, golden and glittering. Others will bottom out at a three, heavy and hard. But when you step back and look at the whole of it, the ups and downs together, it averages out. 7 out of 10 is actually a very generous slice of life.

If your day didn't go perfectly, but you got a good cup of coffee and a kind word, well, that's something golden. If a visit didn't go quite the way you dreamed, but there was a moment of shared laughter or understanding, that's the part to hold close.

We humans are so very good at making wish lists in our heads, aren't we? We imagine the ideal conversation, the spotless kitchen, the uninterrupted afternoon, a friend who always knows just what to say. And when life gives us only parts and pieces, only 7 out of 10, we sometimes call it a failure. But it isn't. It's just life being what life has always been. Messy, beautiful, ordinary, sanctified.

I don't expect perfection from people anymore. I don't even expect it from myself, which has brought me more peace than I ever thought possible. I try, I show up. I bake the cake, even if it sinks in the middle. I write the letter, even if it's a week late. I forgive, even if I have to do it bit by bit by bit. And when others fall short, as they do from time to time, I try to leave a little room for grace. I try to assume good intentions. I try to let people be who they are.

You don't need to have it all to have enough. You don't need to be everything to be good. 7 out of 10 might not be the whole pie, but oh, my dear, it's still so much pie! And what a blessing that is.

So today may I gently suggest this: Expect less. Not in a sad way, but in a soft, merciful way. Expect less of yourself and expect less of others. And in that gentle space, you might just find that you're surrounded by more sweetness than you realized.

Let your shoulders drop, my dear. You're doing just fine.

Unrushed, Unapologetic

I used to have one of those coffee makers that used the little plastic pod thingies. It belonged to my youngest son Noah, and he took it with him when he moved out, many years ago now. These days I make my morning coffee in a 1930s Dripolator coffee maker. There's something so centering and sentimental and unrushed about making coffee this way. She's a cheerful little thing, enameled in soft cream with faded red apples tumbling across her sides like something from an old kitchen calendar. The handle has darkened from years of careful holding, and there's the faintest little hairline crack on the lid, like a wrinkle that tells you she's been around long enough to know things.

It's not the kind of coffee you make quickly. No buttons, no hums or pings. You boil the water separately—on the stove, of course, while the house is still quiet and the windows are fogged from sleep. Then you pour the water slowly into the top compartment of the coffeepot, where it trickles its way down through the grounds on its own good time. No rushing her, she drips *plip, plip, plip*, like rainfall against a tin roof. Steady and soft. There are lots of steps, a lot of waiting, but I love how it fills my whole kitchen with a rich coffee aroma. I love how pretty it is.

It certainly is slow, but it's the good kind of slow. The kind that gives you a moment to breathe, to glance out the kitchen window and notice the way the sunlight lands on the porch rail, the kind of waiting that lets you hear the kittens padding around or the ticktick of the old wall clock.

I've always been slow. I was the slowest runner in my gym class every year of high school, and I'm even slower-moving now. I'm slow to accept change. I'm slow to anger, slow to lose faith. I take my time, and I take time for others. Speed is a beautiful thing. And efficiency can be helpful, but slow is nice too.

It really is okay to be the exact person you were created to be, my darlings. I used to dislike how slow and plodding I am, but now I see that some of my favorite things about myself are part of that slowness. I've learned to take joy and comfort in the balance.

So I pour a cup of coffee, take it to my favorite chair, and sip it slowly too. Some things just aren't meant to be hurried.

Not Lazy, Just Different

Growing up, I was called lazy so many times that I began to believe it. "Lazy" felt like a settled fact about me. Not something to question, just something to carry. But over the years, I've learned a softer truth: Sometimes what looks like laziness from the outside is simply exhaustion. For some of us, especially in certain seasons of life, just surviving, just doing the bare minimum, uses up every last drop of energy we have.

Others looking in might not understand why the garden goes wild, why the dishes pile up, why the homework never quite . . . gets . . . finished. They might label us lazy. But now I can look back on those hard seasons with more compassion. I see that I wasn't weak or flawed. I was doing my best. And though my best was quiet and modest, sometimes invisible to others, it was still strength.

These days I have more time and more energy. I even garden, or rather, my own silly version of it. I've never managed to keep plants alive for very long, but I'm forever buying pots of flowers grown and nurtured by steadier hands. I replant them in cheerful groupings, tuck fairy garden trinkets among the stems, arrange them in old wicker stands and chipped metal racks. I fill the porch, the windowsills, and I will them to bloom as long as their sweet little green heart's desire.

I used to think I was too lazy for gardening, but maybe I just needed to find my own way into it. And maybe I needed to be kind enough to myself to let my way be a *good enough* way.

There are so many things I once believed I couldn't do when in truth I just hadn't found the grace or space to do them in my own way and in my own time. I wish I could go back and be gentler with myself during those hard years. I can't. *You* can't. But I can choose gentleness now. And I can encourage you, my darling, to do the same. Your way, however slow, however small, however different, is good enough.

Be Kind to Yourself

People sometimes ask if I've always been the way I am now. And in many ways, the answer is yes. I've always been slow and plodding. I've always been quick to smile, always loved to laugh. I've always loved old things, slow things, comforting things. I've always had my little ways and vintage ways. But one big difference, I think, is that I used to be nicer.

When I was younger, I took pride in being nice. I liked being seen as agreeable, pleasant, the sort of person who'd never make waves.

Nice, after all, is easy to admire. But somewhere along the way, I came to understand something deeper: Nice isn't always the same as good. Nice often seeks approval, while kind seeks connection. Nice wants to be liked; kind wants to do what's right. Nice says the polite thing, even if it isn't quite true. Kind finds a way to tell the truth, but gently. Niceness can be a performance; kindness requires presence. And most of all, kindness asks something of us. It asks us to step outside ourselves. To soften when we could snap. To listen when we want to lecture. To try, even when we're tired.

Which brings me to another question I get sometimes: Why do I talk so often about being kind to yourself? Isn't it more important to be kind to others?

Well, here's the truth: I spent a long time being hard on myself. I thought that if I just scolded myself enough, I'd shape up. If I punished myself for every mistake, I'd eventually become someone worthy. But it didn't work.

Being hard on myself didn't make me better. It made me bitter. It made me brittle. It made me less available to others, not more. It wasn't until I learned to forgive myself that I could really extend that forgiveness to anyone else. When I reminded myself of my strengths, those strengths grew. When I let myself rest, I had the energy to care. When I treated myself with gentleness, I became gentle.

I remember a time when Millen and I were out for lunch. We couldn't help but notice a young woman at the next table, elegant, striking, wearing a bright pink hat with flowers all around the brim. Millen, who adores hats and wears one every day, couldn't take her eyes off it.

But as we watched, it became clear that her loveliness didn't extend to her manners. She was curt and dismissive with the waitress, sent her burger back, and rolled her eyes in exaggerated displeasure. When we got up to leave, she pushed past us as we approached our car, knocking Millen's hat to the ground. I was instantly furious. I wanted to scold her, to demand an apology for my darling girl. But I didn't.

Instead, I picked up the hat, brushed it off, and handed it to Millen with a smile. Then I turned to the young woman and said, "My daughter has been admiring your hat all through lunch. It's just beautiful."

She paused. Didn't look at me. But as she got into her car, she stopped to touch the magnet on my car door. It reads: *Everything will turn out in the end.*

"I saw that when I parked," she murmured. Then she got in and drove away. And I saw that she was crying.

Kindness, my dear ones, has a way of slipping past our defenses. It nudges open doors that anger might slam shut. I don't know what that woman was going through, but I know what she needed wasn't more harshness. It was grace. It was the gentleness for others I learned by treating myself kindly.

So yes, kindness matters. It matters when you're looking in the mirror. It matters when you're talking to someone who's struggling, and it matters when the person struggling is you.

Kindness might cost you something. But oh, my darlings, the return on that investment is immeasurable.

Be kind. Be tender. Not because it will make people like you but because it will make the world a little more bearable. A little more beautiful. A little more like home.

For Every Kind of Girl

Well, my dears, I recently heard of some folks, bless their hearts, going out of their way to make fun of women who shave. Or maybe it was women who don't shave. Or maybe it was just women who have to shave? Some silliness about whiskers and femininity and what a real woman should or shouldn't do.

And all I could think was *Oh, for heaven's sake!*

Let me say this plainly and with all the softness I can muster. Whether you shave your face or not, whether you have a few stray whiskers or a full five o'clock shadow, you are no less feminine. You are not less of a woman, not even a little bit.

There is no one way to be a woman. Some women paint their nails every week, and some never do. Some wear heels, others wear boots. Some bake bread from scratch, some pick it up from the bakery, and some don't like bread at all. Some women have beards, and guess what? They're still women. Fully, beautifully, undeniably.

To all my trans sisters, you are every bit as real, every bit as worthy, and every bit as womanly as any of us. Your presence, your beauty, your truth: it's all welcome here. You do not need to perform femininity a certain way to earn your place. You already belong. If you are tired, if you are weary from having to prove yourself over and over again, come rest here. You are enough.

And to my cis sisters, especially those who've grown up under the harsh gaze of impossible standards: Maybe you were told, directly or subtly, that you had to fit into a narrow little box, that your body needed fixing, or that your womanhood depended on how quietly you behaved, how you wore your hair, how you kept up appearances. Let me whisper to you too. You've always been enough. You don't have to compete or compare with anyone else.

We don't have to understand every experience to make space for another woman's reality,

We're not here to gatekeep, we're here to gather close.

Being a woman isn't something that can be undone by a little facial hair or upheld by a tube of lipstick. It lives deeper than that. It's in your spirit, in your care, in the way you love and live and show up in the world as yourself.

So *pooh* to the meanies! Let them fuss and frown and miss out on the joy of knowing you.

And to you, my dear, whoever you are, if you ever doubt yourself, don't. You are lovely just as you are.

Crooked Stitches and Tiny Knots

I have an old tablecloth that is covered almost completely covered with rows and rows of tiny cross-stitched embroidery. Sometimes I find myself standing at the table, running my fingers gently over the soft weave of this old linen tablecloth, so carefully and patiently made by hands many, many years ago. I often wonder about those hands. Whose were they? What were their lives like? What did they dream about during the long hours they pulled needle and thread through fabric over and over, creating beauty one tiny stitch at a time?

I imagine them fretting just a little over small mistakes, a stitch pulled a little bit too tight, a thread knotted where it shouldn't be, a petal slightly askew, a pattern that didn't quite line up. I can see them leaning in close, sighing softly, worrying whether anyone would notice. That one misplaced rosebud? Or that corner where the design sits just a hair off center?

But here I am, all these years later, and do you know what I see when I look at this cloth? I see devotion, care, love poured out in quiet, patient moments. I see not a list of errors but the marks of a human soul. Those tiny imperfections are not flaws at all. They are fingerprints, proof that this piece was made by someone real, someone who kept stitching even when the thread tangled or the pattern slipped. Someone who picked this tablecloth up time and time and time again. Who made the choice to forgive herself the little mistakes and come back once again to do her best. And that, my dear one, is what makes it so very precious.

Perfection is an illusion we chase but never truly capture. And if we did—if every stitch were mathematically correct, if every line aligned with mechanical precision—wouldn't we lose something in the process? Wouldn't the soul slip quietly out the back door?

It's the same with ourselves, isn't it? We carry our own little knots and crooked stitches. The choices we regret, the habits we wish we could break, the scars we've earned along the way. These are the marks of a life fully lived. Our flaws are not evidence of failure. They are evidence of courage. They are the places where we kept going. Even when it would have been easier to give up. They are the texture of our individuality.

The truth is, what we often see as flaws are exactly the things that make us beautiful to those who love us. The way your voice catches when you're nervous. The stubborn curl in your hair that refuses to be tamed. The laugh that is just a little too loud in quiet places. The quiet word you offered after you lost your temper. The apology you made when you stumbled.

All of it. All of you, precious beyond measure.

The next time you find yourself fretting over your own small mistakes, my darling, I hope you will think of that old tablecloth. I hope you will remember that it is not in spite of its imperfections that it is beautiful. It is *because* of them. And so it is with you.

Embrace Your Inner Weirdo

Wear the thing that makes you feel like a walking daydream.

Speak in tangents. Laugh too loud.

Cry when the leaves change colors.

Cry for children you've never met.

Pray for their heartbroken mothers.

Collect old catalogs. Or rocks. Or facts about sea creatures.

Keep the key to a diary you lost twenty years ago.

Tell stories out of order. Arrange your books by mood.

Hang quilts as curtains. Fill the air in your home with beautiful smells and ridiculous music.

Ask questions that make people blink.

Accept odd looks with a smile. Choose grace, even when it's undeserved.

Assume kindness when you can. And when you can't, respond as if you still believe in it.

Say what you mean. Mean what you say.

Love what you love with your whole entire heart.

Be a little much. Be a lot much!

Be not quite what they expected.

You are not here to blend in.

You are here to bloom.

And the world is better, so much better, because of your peculiar, particular light.

We Don't Fall Down

Do you remember those old children's toy figures, Weebles? Roly-poly little egg-shaped figures with silly little faces, weighted on the bottom. With a touch of a finger, they'd rock hilariously from side to side, always righting themselves in the end. Their little jingle went, "Weebles wobble, but they don't fall down." I always thought that was such a charming idea.

Sometimes I jokingly refer to myself as *Weeble-esque*, because the truth is, I do look rather like a Weeble: nice and round, a little roly-poly, soft around the edges. And I'm okay with that. More than okay, really. I love it.

When I poke fun at my figure or my age or my weight, I promise you I'm not being critical or unkind to myself. Even when I use words like *old* or *chubby* or even *fat*, I'm simply describing myself. Those words carry no venom for me, no sharp edges. They're just words. Simple as that.

Over the years, I've noticed how my roly-poly little figure and my age might influence the style choices I make, but they don't limit them. Not one bit. I wear my hair the way I do and I dress the way I do because those choices feel like me. They express something true about who I am, and that gives me joy.

In a world so full of pressure to look a certain way or chase impossible standards, the kindest thing we can do for ourselves is just relax. To step outside of all the noise and just let our bodies be what they are. Not perfect, not a project. Just enough.

My body is mine. It carries me through the days. It holds my heart, my stories, my ordinary little moments. And that is more than enough.

So if you see me wobbling a little, just know I'm still standing, still smiling. Still showing up exactly as I am.

How to Deal with Meanies

My children have been some of my very best teachers.

One day, when Noah was three or four years old, he showed me something I've never forgotten: how to deal with meanies.

We had a next-door neighbor who struggled in many areas, especially kindness. Even though she was a grown woman, she often shouted at the little ones in the neighborhood. Berated their mamas. She'd call the police on strangers passing by . . . and the code enforcer on the poor neighbor unlucky enough to let his grass get a bit too high or leave his garbage cans out an hour too long. She'd even chase away the hungry stray cats, bless her heart. She was just plain mean to nearly everyone.

Well, one afternoon, Noah was playing happily in the backyard with his little trucks and some sticks and stones, making roads and mountains, completely absorbed in his work. I was watching from the kitchen window when I saw that neighbor approach the edge of our property. I couldn't hear what she said, but her posture, her hands, the stiff line of her jaw, made it clear she was being unkind.

But Noah just looked up at her, smiling. Not a fake or fearful smile but a sweet, open one. He looked at her like she was a curious butterfly who had landed on the edge of his sandbox.

Just as I was about to open the window to intervene, she threw her hands in the air and stalked off. Noah went right back to playing.

"Noah," I called, "was she being mean to you, honey?"

He shrugged and said, "Well, she tried to be mean. But my happy was stronger than her mean. So I won."

And honestly, I think about that moment more often than I can say. Because life is full of meanies. People who lash out because they are hurting or scared or simply haven't yet learned how to love. And while it's important to stand up for ourselves and protect our peace, it's also true that sometimes—not always, but sometimes—we can quietly hold our joy like a shield. And that shield can be surprisingly strong.

Noah wasn't trying to win. He wasn't trying to teach a lesson. He was simply rooted in his own little contented world, and her storm couldn't rattle him.

So when you encounter a meanie—a real, honest-to-goodness grump who wants to pull you into their unhappiness—take a breath. Feel your feet on the ground. Remember what you love. Keep your happy strong.

A Morning That Is Mine

Folks often ask me about my morning routine, but to be honest, I'm not sure if I have a morning routine.

Of course, I do always get up, but the time varies from day to day. Some mornings I wash my face right away, and other times it waits until a few other things are done first. I'm always so happy to look out my windows and check the weather. That simple glance is like taking the temperature of the day, feeling its mood, and whispering a little hello to the sky.

I always get a few pleasant little chores done. The cats must be fed, of course. Those kittens don't miss a meal. I usually spend a few moments tidying things up, but full disclosure, I almost never do any real cleaning first thing in the morning. The energy for scrubbing and fussing just hasn't arrived yet, and that's perfectly fine.

One of my very favorite morning chores is freshening my flowers, but I don't do that every day either. Still, when I do, oh, what joy. A little snip here, a gentle fluff there. It feels like setting the stage for kindness.

My mornings flow gently and change from day to day, like a little stream that curves around the rocks of daily life. I try to get outside in the very early morning. I try to walk a few laps in my driveway for the exercise and fresh air. I'd love to be able to go on a hike on a pristine nature trail or maybe even take a leisurely stroll through the village to a favorite coffee shop. But doing laps in my teensy little driveway is what I've got right now. And it's plenty good enough.

I walk around my son Noah's lovely vintage car, which lives in my driveway. I listen to the birds, I feel the cool breeze, and it gives me so much joy. Sometimes I can watch the sunrise, and those are the very best mornings.

Once inside again, I usually light my morning candle. Just a little beeswax tea light, just enough light to show off a pretty little picture postcard in the back of the candle stand, just enough glow to remind me that light is always waiting to be kindled again.

Of course not every morning is this soft and open. Some mornings are busier, when I need to be somewhere or prepare for company or dive into a full list of tasks. On those days I move with more purpose, but the constants remain the same.

Every morning I have my coffee. Every morning I have my Sit and Stare Time, and every morning I think of my community online.

That's my morning routine, or lack thereof. It's not glamorous or disciplined or worthy of a glossy magazine layout, but it's mine. And in its flexibility, it gives me the space to meet the day as I am. If I wake cheerful and full of energy, I can bustle about. If I wake weary, I can move slowly and gently. Always, I pause to notice something beautiful, to sip my coffee and let it remind me of steadiness and warmth. That little moment becomes my touchstone, the small strength I can carry with me into whatever the day holds.

And I hope whatever shape your mornings take, you feel that steadiness too.

Eat the Berries Yourself

When my children were small, our grocery budget was always stretched a little too tight. There wasn't room for many treats or trifles. But almost every week I managed to find a way to buy one little basket of berries. Just one.

I chose it carefully, turning each container over to inspect the bottom, gently checking the fruit for bruises. I looked for the basket that seemed to sparkle the most, the one that whispered a promise of sweetness. Blueberries in July, raspberries in September, out-of-season (and outrageously expensive) strawberries in January. Each morning I'd count out the berries onto my children's plate, one by one, making sure it was even, stretching that tiny luxury as far as it could possibly go.

Back then, berries were for them, always for them. It never even occurred to me to set a few aside for me.

And now, things are easier. My grocery budget isn't so tight. I usually buy a couple of baskets every week. I only have Millen to feed, and even when I heap her plate with fruit, those berries often linger in the fridge a little too long. Some weeks they soften, they spoil, they get thrown out.

It hit me one afternoon, staring down a shriveled raspberry at the back of the fridge: *I could have eaten that. I* should *have eaten that!*

Old habits are funny. We do the same things long after they stop making sense. We stretch and sacrifice and give, and sometimes we forget that we're allowed to receive too. That kindness isn't only meant to flow outward; we are not the exception to our own tenderness.

For years, I believed that it was somehow noble to neglect myself, that it was virtuous to always come last. That I could bully or deprive myself into becoming a better person. But, my dear, I've learned that cruelty and neglect don't create growth. Not in others and not in ourselves.

So here's what I'm learning: It's okay to want nice things. It's okay to have nice things. It's okay to treat yourself with the same sweetness you offer your most beloved ones.

If you are working hard to love others well, to keep them safe and seen and cherished, then please remember you are worthy of those things too. You are not the exception, and you are not the afterthought.

You are the one standing in the kitchen measuring out love with every spoonful.

Let some of it be for you.

Eat the berries, my darling.

Buy the dress.

Light the candle.

Pour the good cream in your coffee.

Tuck the pretty napkin onto your own lap.

You don't need to earn kindness.

You only need to remember you are someone worth loving too.

A Little Water, a Little Care

Some kinds of care are quiet and simple and easy, like fluffing the pillows on someone's favorite chair or smiling at that frazzled young mother in the grocery store. Holding the door for that gentleman with his armload of packages. Some kinds of care are quieter still, like slipping on warm socks before your feet hit the cold floor or remembering to stretch your stiff legs before the day begins. They may seem small, even boring, but these tiny acts are threads that can hold a whole life together.

But the simplest things can be the hardest sometimes, can't they? For example, I've always had such a hard time remembering to water the flowers on my front porch.

This summer I've added the task to my early-morning chore list. Each evening I make sure the watering cans are filled, and each morning I take my roly-poly little self out to the front porch. The kittens have already been fed about an hour before, and they're off making mischief. It's just the old folks, cats, and me, and I think they appreciate the fresh cool air as much as the flowers appreciate their water.

Another one of the simplest little tasks, and somehow one of the trickiest for me, is just remembering to take my meds. It sounds so basic, doesn't it? But I so often used to forget. These days, I make it easy. I place them in a pretty little dish on my kitchen counter, right in the heart of my morning routine. And just like the porch plants, I've bloomed a little more each day with that small act of consistency.

Watering flowers is care. Taking your meds is care. It's not glamorous, it's not thrilling, but, my darling, it matters.

Sometimes love looks like refilling the watering can the night before. Sometimes it looks like swallowing your pills on time. We so often pour out for others, but don't forget to pour in too.

Your well-being is worth tending. And just like those flowers, you'll grow and bloom best when you're lovingly looked after. So take your medicine, drink your water, and let someone, even if it's just you, care for you.

I'll be thinking of you today and hoping for wonderful, steady things.

I Love Monday Mornings

Ordinary mornings are my favorite.

Summer can be so incredibly busy. Day trips, weekend jaunts, several batches of houseguests, some staying for weeks at a time. And oh, how much fun we have. Spirited chats over morning coffee, the excitement of new things to share with old friends nearly every day. I love every minute of it.

But there's something so soothing, so satisfying, so healing about waking up knowing there are no extra demands on you for the day, taking your time. And some pleasant little chores just to make things pretty. Setting aside a few minutes to bake something sweet and special just the way your most beloved ones like it. Making your coffee just the way you like it yourself.

Let's just take a minute and start our day together. I love a nice strong cup of coffee with cream, and I make a point of having real cream. There are times to sacrifice and cut corners, to be sure. There are instant coffee mornings, skipped breakfast mornings, the last-of-the-skim-milk mornings. But in my opinion, the first thing one takes in the morning, especially a Monday morning, is the moment to indulge just a little bit. For me, it's cream. Maybe for you it's a bit of sugar. Maybe it's a drop or two of maple syrup stirred gently into your cup. Maybe it's getting that fancy drink from the drive-through that makes you feel a little more like yourself.

Or maybe it's simply rinsing out your very favorite mug, the one that feels just right in your hands, the one that gives you comfort. Whatever it is, I dearly hope you indulge yourself just a little this morning, and not just this morning but always.

There are some days when we pour ourselves out for others. And yes, those are glorious, joyful days. But if you can, don't forget to balance those busy mornings with quiet mornings, ordinary days when you can focus on your most important job: taking good care of yourself.

Exciting, busy days are wonderful and so fun. But I love my quiet, ordinary mornings best of all.

I remember a time when I used to dread Monday mornings. I had to fight to see anything hopeful coming in the week ahead. But times change, our lives and circumstances change. And nothing, my dear, is forever.

These days, Monday morning is my favorite.

I've got my little kitty companions, a pretty little cottage to live in, beautiful warm clothes to wear. Monday mornings now feel like the beginning of a whole fresh week to fill with lovely, happy things.

But even on those hard, hard Monday mornings years ago, no matter how rushed I was, I'd always take a few minutes to sit with my coffee. A few minutes to find something beautiful to focus on, a few minutes to calm my racing heart. Things aren't always easy, my dear one, I know that. But taking time for yourself, even a few small minutes can make the hardest days just a little bit softer. I'm thinking of you this morning, honey, hoping that in the middle of your morning rush, you'll take the time to care for beautiful, precious you.

Ordinary Things

Sometimes
the most ordinary things
are the most beautiful
like the morning sun
shining though the leaves
of the tree in my backyard
glinting through my dining room window
glowing in the petals of the hydrangeas
I picked from the front garden
I promise you
there is beauty
all around you
my dear one
I hope you can see it today
I hope it strengthens you
and I hope it gives you joy
Wishing you beauty today
my dear one
beauty
and strength
and joy

The Magic of Odd Friendships

They don't always look like you expect. Odd friendships, I mean. Sometimes they begin with a shared smile over the last lemon tart at a bakery. Or a neighbor who returns your stray cat (again) and ends up sitting with you on the porch for hours. Sometimes they form between people with nothing in common but a shared appreciation for the sound of wind through the trees.

Odd friendships can look like a twenty-year age gap. Like one of you wearing vintage lace and the other in a motorcycle jacket. One of you quoting poetry and the other telling off-color jokes. They bloom anyway, somehow.

They often start quietly. Not with fireworks or declarations but with a casual, "Need help with that?" or "Is that a 1940s tablecloth? My grandmother had one just like it."

They grow in the cracks where you least expect them. You share a little. Then a little more. You discover a shared fondness for lemon soap or 1970s British mysteries. You begin to look forward to their knock on your door or their video call at 10 P.M. You text each other weird things when you should be working. You exchange soup recipes and talk about what you're afraid of. You laugh until your faces hurt.

And somehow, this person who was once a stranger is now woven into the fabric of your life.

There's something beautiful about loving someone who is completely different from you. It stretches your understanding. It opens your heart. Odd friendships are where growth happens. Where laughter bubbles up unexpectedly. Where you are reminded that connection doesn't come from similarity but from tenderness. From appreciation.

The world would like us to believe we should seek only those who reflect us. But I think there is magic in choosing to love someone whose life is nothing like our own.

Take my dear friend Rebecca, for example. We have led such incredibly different lives. And our days are completely different still, with different styles and different ways of expressing ourselves. But somehow, every time we talk, I come away feeling seen and celebrated. We share stories, send each other odd bits of inspiration, and make one another laugh in that deep, soul-shaking way that feels like medicine. She reminds me that friendship doesn't have to look like a matching pair—it can look like contrast, like a patchwork quilt of two very different but deeply kindred spirits.

So here's to the odd friendships. The surprising ones. The lovely mismatched duos who sit on porches and swap stories and hand each other tissues and casseroles. May we cherish them always.

May we be brave enough to make more.

The Precious Person Is You

What are you waiting for,
my darling?
You're saving all the pretty things,
the special things.
They're tucked away in drawers,
pushed to the back of the cabinet,
away up on a special shelf,
away even where your eyes
don't have the pleasure of them.
What are you waiting for,
my dear?
Are you waiting for a special day,
a special event,
an elusive person
precious enough
for your precious things?
Use the pretty things,
my dear.
Eat the candy,
pour out the heavy cream.
You don't need to wait.
The special day is today.
The special event is life.
The precious person
is you.

On Change

I've never been especially fond of change. But over the years, I've gotten better at walking through it with grace.

Now summer is giving way to fall. The mornings are no longer golden and warm but dusky and cool. The air has changed. The light has shifted.

And change, well . . . it's still not easy. But I've learned not to dwell too long on what I'm leaving behind. Instead, I gently turn my gaze toward the good things ahead. Because no matter how much I'll miss what's slipping away, there's always something waiting. Always something new that will bring joy, if I'm willing to let it.

When my youngest son moved into his own beautiful new home, I'm not going to lie, it was quite an adjustment for this mama. That first night, I cried and cried. The next morning, I woke up feeling a bit lost. The house was too quiet. Too still.

But I was happy for him. I was proud of him. And I was determined to make the best of this change.

His last week at home became a week of tender little goodbyes. The last Monday morning, I rose before dawn and made him breakfast in a dusky kitchen. The last time I heard his footsteps on the stairs in the early morning. The last time we sat on the porch together after dinner.

But it was also a week of firsts. This morning, I slept until the sun shining through my bedroom window woke me. This evening, for the first time in a while, I had the time and energy to clean my French doors, and, silly as it may sound, it was deeply satisfying. I've started to imagine this new season as a blank page, waiting to be filled.

Sadness and joy can exist together like two currents in the same stream. Loneliness and hope, it's a kind of dance. We learn to acknowledge the difficult moments, to let them speak their piece, while still giving space for joy to take our hand and lead us forward.

Because change can be both exciting and terrifying. It can fill us with energy and drain us all at once. Sometimes, it makes us feel in control. Other times, it reminds us just how little control we really have.

But one thing we always have a say in is how we respond.

For me, that means not ignoring the pain but also not feeding it. It means noticing the beauty that remains, the good that still exists. It means allowing myself to be excited about what's ahead, even while I'm grieving what I've left behind.

If you're facing a change right now, my dear one, I hope it's the kind that stirs joy and adventure. But even if it isn't, I hope you can still spot the glimmers of beauty tucked into your days. I hope joy finds you and keeps you company.

Because even in the hardest seasons, there is always something to look forward to. Always something new to love.

Summer's End

It's still summer, but there's a touch of autumn in the air. The sun rises later. It's dusky and cool when I first get up. My beloved roses and pansies are long since gone, but clematis and mums are not too far ahead. My cozy, woolen lace shawl has come out of storage and warms me as I watch the late-summer sunrise. Change is hard, but it helps me to think of specific things ahead that will give me joy—not ignoring the anxiety of leaving the familiar and beloved things behind but balancing that with the sure and certain knowledge that the uncertain things ahead will become familiar and beloved in their time.

Autumn

*Autumn teaches us the grace of release.
Leaves flame and fall, reminding us
that letting go can be beautiful too.
The air sharpens, and we gather what the
year has grown, even as we prepare to lay aside
what no longer serves us. These essays
are harvest reflections: moments of gratitude,
reckoning, and the tender courage of change.*

Even Just One Lovely Thing

These days,
loveliness is all around me.
It greets me in the morning light,
waits for me in the quiet corners
of my home.

But that wasn't always so.
I remember the ache of old mornings—
sitting in my car,
holding my coffee like a shield,
waiting until the last possible moment
to step into a job
that drained the joy from me.

Some days,
thc only beauty I knew
was the warmth through the paper cup,
or the way rain danced
softly on my windshield.

Still—
those tiny fragments of lovely
sustained me.
They reminded me
that beauty hadn't vanished,
only hidden.

And so this morning,
I hope you are surrounded

by things that make your heart sigh
with gladness.

But if you're not—
if beauty feels far away today—
then I hope you can find
just one small, shining thing.
Even the tiniest lovely moment
can be enough
to carry you through

even if only
just enough.

Bright Little Jewels

Some days are hard, but some days are not. Some days are easy and bright. Some days your hair looks every bit as pretty as you hoped. Some days the sweet new dress fits just right. Some days you have the perfect shoes. Some days the rain stops, and all the flowers are covered with glittering little raindrop jewels.

Save those days. Save up those perfect little moments. Preserve them in your mind.

Take up that little wisp of your darling baby's hair and tuck it between the pages of a beautiful book. Make a scrapbook of old tickets and receipts from that special dinner out. Press a flower you picked on that glorious autumn morning walk. Don't let your beautiful moments and bright sunny days slip away—make a point to remember them and store them away in your mind and heart. One day you'll have your absolute best cup of coffee. One day you'll read the very best chapter of what will become your favorite book, maybe even on the same day if you're very lucky.

Remember those days. Save them up like jewels.

In the midst of hard times or depression, it can feel as though joy will never return, but that bank account of joyful memories can encourage you and give you hope even on your darkest days. When the hard days return, pull those bright, happy jewels out. Let them remind you that hard times are not all of your life, that you're also meant for beautiful, happy days, and they will come to you again.

These days, my life is mostly happy and bright. Mostly. But, my darlings, the truth is that every life has its challenges. Even the easiest phases of life include heartbreak.

Every day, I am missing loved ones who are far away and out of my reach. As I write these words, one of my dearest and most precious relationships is currently full of strife and contention. One year when everything was sailing beautifully along, with success and love at the end of every fingertip, I was suddenly faced with some very scary health concerns.

But if even the easiest times have difficulties, it is equally true that even the most difficult times have beauty. And joy.

So much happens that we have little control over, but even in the midst of challenging times, there is one thing I will always have control over: my thoughts.

I have a little box in my heart, my dears, a box where I've stored up happy thoughts; remembrances of beautiful moments, comforting things I know are true. Bright little jewels.

It may feel as though our lives are controlled by those challenging things that make life so hard, but that's not true. As hard and as real as hard times are, these bright little jewels are every bit as real. Every bit as powerful.

Your feelings will grow from the thoughts you choose. Your feelings will direct your actions, and your actions will become your life.

So today, let me encourage you to think powerful, strengthening, happy thoughts. Make a joyful memory today, my dear one.

You are strong, my darling. You are brave and beautiful. You have a wonderfully exciting future. You are safe.

Unlearning Perfect

Nobody's perfect, but I do suspect that I might be more imperfect than most. I'm chubby. I have raging ADHD, which means my thoughts are often darting around like butterflies at a garden party: lovely, but nearly impossible to wrangle. I have high ideals and grand ambitions. But I all too often falter in the nitty-gritty of the follow-through. My baseboards are never quite clean enough. I allow my daughter Millen more screen time than is strictly advisable. And heaven knows I allow myself far more screen time than any adult woman reasonably should! I freely acknowledge my imperfections. I laugh at myself often, and I do so with love. But somehow, in the tangled logic of my mind, none of this has ever stopped me from being a perfectionist.

Isn't that wild?

For years—decades really—I held myself to impossible standards in my appearance, in my work, in my home. Every detail had to be thought out, polished, managed. Everything needed to be perfect. And of course, it never was, because nothing can be. And so nothing was ever good enough. I was never good enough. And that is the curse of perfectionism. It looks like ambition, but it feels like failure.

These days I am aiming for something entirely different. These days I aim for beauty.

And you know what? Beauty is so much easier to reach.

I find it in the fluttering of curtains by my open bedroom windows, in the soft rustle of leaves on the maple tree I see while washing my face in the morning. I come downstairs and find it in the golden spill of sunlight across my not-quite-dusted but pleasant living room. A worn old scarf draped across the fireplace mantle. A chipped enamel coffeepot sitting cheerfully on the stove. A jadeite tray with a single candle flickering.

Nothing is perfect, but oh, it's all so beautiful.

There is such a soft, quiet release in learning to appreciate the beauty of imperfect things, in loving our homes, our people, and our own complicated selves as they are. If you come by my house and see a wrinkled tablecloth, a patch on my dress, a little dust on the shelves, I do hope you'll understand. I've stopped striving for perfect. I'm happy, deeply happy, to settle for beautiful.

I used to be embarrassed by a particular tablecloth I often hid when guests came by. She's a faded, threadbare thing with holes that grow a little bigger every time I wash her. There are old scorch marks from long-ago Sunday roasts, still dark and distinct from the days when she lived in someone else's ragbag. I rescued her from a church rummage sale 40 years ago, and I still remember the way I held her up and thought, *Well, you've got some life left in you.*

And oh, she has lived.

She charms me to this day with her perfectly faded shades of blue, pink, and soft green. Pink scalloped edges, flowers of uncertain identity. Are they roses? Tulips? Possibly strawberries? Fat blueberries nestled beside them, and that fabric—thick, soft cotton so hard to find in linens today. She has seen so many meals, heard so many stories, felt the elbows and hands of so many beloveds. She belongs here, in my home, among all the other flawed things in my cupboards and in my life.

I no longer feel embarrassed by her flaws. I feel affection, reverence even. The worn and well-loved things are my favorites now. They remind me that beauty is not in the absence of wear but in the evidence of it. Beauty is the proof that something has been used. Loved, trusted, lived with.

I'm a recovering perfectionist, yes, but not in the defeated, discouraged kind of way. No, I've simply decided that perfect is no longer the prize. Beauty is. And beauty is everywhere when you know where to look, when you let your heart soften toward the chipped, the stained, the weathered, the worn. When you let your life, your home, yourself be real.

These days you'll find me with a little cracked vase of pale tulips on the table, one petal starting to curl. A single tea light burning low. My beloved tablecloth laid out with care and no apologies. And the most glorious cup of coffee you've ever tasted.

I'm no longer chasing perfection, my darling. I'm just here, content, settling for beautiful.

Gifts in Disappointment

When we first moved into this house, I'll be honest with you, my heart sank the moment I walked into the kitchen. The entire space had been sponge-painted in an odd and almost aggressive mixture of bright pastels, periwinkle, neon, lavender, baby pink, all spattered thickly over the backdrop of landlord-special white. It wasn't just the walls either. The woodwork, the cupboards. It wasn't pretty. It wasn't cozy. It didn't match the bright fruit-covered vintage kitchen curtains I was determined to hang up. It wasn't me *at all.*

But even that somehow wasn't the worst of it. The countertops nearly did me in: dismal brownish-gray, battered and stained from years of use. They looked so old and cracked and scratched, I wasn't even sure if they were still sanitary. And the worst part? There was no changing them. We rent. And even if we owned the house, the cost of new kitchen counters would have been simply out of reach.

I was so disappointed. More than disappointed, really. I felt helpless. I wanted this house to feel like ours, but I didn't have the means to make it what I had envisioned.

Still, we did what we could. The landlord pretty much gave us free rein. We could paint whatever we wanted, fix what needed fixing, as long as we footed the bill ourselves. The kids and I painted the kitchen walls a soft calming gray. We brightened up the woodwork and cupboards with lots of clean, cheerful white paint. With just those changes, the room began to feel lighter, more like a space that could welcome us. But the countertops, those dang countertops remained.

Eventually, though, I began to let my imagination run wild. I can't replace these counters, but what else can I do? One day while grocery shopping, I found rolls of gingham contact paper in the loveliest shade of pale blue-green. It felt like such a small thing, almost silly at the time, but as I carefully laid that impulse-bought paper across the tired old counters, something surprising happened. The room transformed. Somehow that contact paper was the perfect match and counterpoint to those vintage curtains I had hung in the windows. Suddenly this kitchen that had once made me sigh with disappointment made me smile instead.

And now I absolutely adore those countertops. The bright, cheerful gingham brings me joy every single day. What was once an eyesore became one of my favorite things about this space.

Life has a funny way of working like that, doesn't it? The disappointments we think we will never get past soften over time. They surprise us. Sometimes, with a little patience and a touch of creativity, they turn into something beautiful.

Of course, my dear, most disappointments are harder to bear than an ugly kitchen, I know that. But if you can keep even a tiny corner of your heart open, open to possibility, open to improvisation, you may just find that the things that once weighed you down are the very things that bring you unexpected joy.

Disappointment isn't the end of the story. Sometimes it's only the beginning of something better than you could have imagined.

Your Worth Is Infinite

Millen joined our family as a newborn, entrusted to us by her birth parents, who didn't feel able to parent a child with Down syndrome. This was our first adoption, and somehow the call came at just the right moment. We traveled for hours to meet them, hearts open and sure, and when I first held her in my arms, I felt it. An unmistakable knowing. There was a quiet magic about her, a light all her own. She felt like someone I had always known, or perhaps more accurately, someone who I had always wanted to know. I didn't yet know how she would change me, how she would reshape my understanding of value and belonging, but I knew I was holding someone extraordinary. Her birth parents named her Millen—"Precious Gift" in their native language in Ethiopia—and never was there a child more aptly named.

Millen has taught me many things, but perhaps the most profound lesson was about worth, the kind of worth that doesn't come from accolades or income or traditional "success." The kind of worth that doesn't need to be earned, proved, or explained.

I grew up in a world that valued productivity. You were what you accomplished. Status, salary, milestones, those were the metrics that determined how valuable someone was. But very early on in Millen's life, I realized those measures wouldn't apply to her in the same way they did for others. She wouldn't have a career. She wouldn't climb corporate ladders or collect degrees. And yet, I saw her worth written on every inch of her being.

Her worth was never in question. Not to me. Not to our family. Not to her sister Amelia, who once said as a child, "We wouldn't be us if it wasn't for Millen." And she was right. Millen has shaped us, softened us, brightened our world in ways I never could have anticipated. She is essential. She has become the center of our family, the center of our lives.

She has taught me how to love unconditionally. How to release judgment and unrealistic standards. How to value others without conditions or caveats. How to receive what others offer with gratitude and grace. How to let their best be enough, and in doing so, how to let my own best be enough.

Years ago, I experienced something called sudden hearing loss. In a single moment, due to nerve damage, I lost most of my hearing and was plunged into a terrifying bout of vertigo. I couldn't open my eyes. I couldn't lift my head from the pillow, not even the thinnest one. I spent weeks in bed, unable to move, speak, or care for myself.

So many people offered help during that painful, disorienting time. But the help that left the deepest mark came from Millen. She simply sat by my side. Quiet. Still. Holding my hand. That was it. She didn't need me to talk or to move. She asked nothing of me. She was simply present. Her small, warm hand in mine said everything: *You are loved. You are not alone. I will stay.*

Tears would spill from the corners of my eyes, silently soaking into the pillow. I had never felt so wholly accepted. So deeply, gently loved. That simple act of presence changed me. When my own father was near death, I followed her example. I sat by his bed. I held his hand. I offered my love without condition or expectation. Through my touch, I told him that he had done enough. That he was enough. Millen taught me how to love like that.

And then there's the matter of cats. Millen has always had a special relationship with animals. Years ago, we had a large black cat named Tilty with vivid green eyes. That cat adored Millen. He'd warm her lap through winter afternoons and let her rest her iPad on his furry belly while she worked on her speech program. They were companions in every sense.

When Tilty passed, we were devastated. But eventually, we decided to welcome another cat. I imagined a replacement, a cat that would follow Millen from room to room, curl into her lap, and purr at her touch.

Instead, we got Caoimhe.

Caoimhe, a dilute ginger cat with golden eyes, had spent her early life isolated and alone in a cage. She was wary, distant, and would flinch from touch. She never purred. She wouldn't come close. I was disappointed, I admit. I'd wanted a cat who loved Millen the way Tilty had.

But Millen—oh, Millen—she never gave up. She'd sit near Caoimhe for hours, speaking in a soft, gentle voice, narrating her day or reciting lines from her favorite videos. Slowly, the cat began to listen. Millen bought treats with her allowance and began offering them from her chair. At first, Caoimhe wouldn't come near. So Millen tossed them gently to the floor. Then a bit closer. Then closer still. Until one day, Caoimhe delicately took a treat from Millen's hand.

"She loves me," she whispered, her face glowing.

That moment changed me too. Because Millen taught me that love doesn't always arrive in the package we expect. It may not be loud or demonstrative. It may not match our ideas of how it should look. But it is no less precious. No less real. And sometimes, it is even more meaningful for its quiet arrival.

Millen doesn't measure her days by productivity. She measures them by joy. By kindness. By connection. And in doing so, she has reminded me again and again that those are the true measures of a life well lived. It doesn't matter if she ever accomplishes anything because she's worth everything.

You are not valuable because of what you achieve. You are not worthy only when you succeed. You are valuable because you exist. Because you love. Because you *are*.

And if no one has told you lately, your worth is infinite. Just as you are.

The Welcoming Presence

For as long as I can remember, Millen has had the rare ability to change the atmosphere of a room simply by entering it. There's no performance to it, no carefully chosen words or practiced gestures. She leads with presence, a kind of quiet, steady warmth that makes people breathe a little easier. Over the years, I've come to understand this as her most profound gift: not just loving people but making them feel profoundly *welcomed.*

When I think about what it means to welcome someone, I think of Millen. Not as an abstract idea but in the thousand small ways she offers this gift in her daily life. There was the time, years ago, when a man stood alone at the back of our church, clearly unsure of his place. As we passed by him, Millen, without hesitation, gently took his hand and said, "Hi. I'm Millen. I'm glad you came." That was it. No preamble. No asking who he was or why he was there. Just a simple offering of presence. It shifted something in me, watching her. It made me rethink every time I'd hesitated to reach out, to include, to make room.

Millen welcomes others not by smoothing over their differences but by honoring them. She doesn't demand they shrink themselves to fit. She simply offers space—real, tender, judgment-free space. You belong, her presence says, exactly as you are.

She's taught me that hospitality isn't about a polished home or the perfect meal. It's about how we make people *feel* in our presence. When I was terribly ill, flattened by vertigo and unable to lift my head, it was Millen who sat beside me hour after hour, holding my hand. She didn't chatter or ask questions. She just stayed. Her quiet companionship became a kind of sanctuary. In that stillness, I understood something I hadn't quite grasped before: that to be truly welcomed is to be accepted without the need to perform or improve. It is to be loved without conditions.

Millen brings this same patience and presence to her relationship with our rescue cat, Caoimhe. A wary, prickly creature, Caoimhe wasn't quick to trust. But Millen, in her gentle and steady way, offered tiny gestures of kindness—soft conversation, scattered treats, open hands. And eventually, love bloomed where it hadn't seemed possible. It reminded me that welcome often looks like patience, like quiet faith that trust will come if we make the space for it.

Being a welcoming person isn't something you perform once in a while. It's a way of being in the world. It's in the way you look at people, the way you hold silence, the way you make room for those who are unsure of their place. It's in the warmth of your yes, in the gentleness of your no, in the presence you offer even when you don't have the right words.

Millen is my daily reminder that kindness is a choice and that welcome is a practice. She's taught me that we can choose to be a place of refuge for one another. We can choose to be a soft place to land.

And so I try, in all my interactions—with friends, with strangers, with those who leave kind comments and those who don't—to let Millen's example guide me. To lead not with cleverness or certainty but with warmth. To say, in a thousand quiet ways: *I'm glad you're here. You matter. You belong.*

Two Ways Back

It doesn't happen often, but when I get angry, I can be very ungracious indeed. Truly, I don't anger easily. Not with strangers, not even with life's everyday irritations. But now and then, something tips the scales. And when that happens, well, let's just say I don't exactly glow with spiritual maturity.

Fortunately, I live in a house where humor is our shared language, especially in moments of tension. Not long ago, I was having a rather dramatic little tantrum about something or other (as one does), and my adult children found it so amusing that they began making photo memes of me mid-rant. One child was in the house, another was across town, and a third was across the ocean. Transcontinental familial hilarity! They texted the memes back and forth until they were practically in tears, then shared them with me. And I, in turn, dissolved into laughter. My storm-cloud mood passed, replaced by that rowdy joy unique to family goofiness. In that moment, I was reminded of something important: humor, when rooted in love, has the power to draw us back to ourselves.

But laughter isn't my only rescue. I'm a single mother of five, and there were long stretches of life when stress was the backdrop to every waking moment. Early mornings. Tight budgets. Childcare drop-offs. A full day of work at a job that drained me. Evenings of homework, dinner, laundry. It was relentless. Back then, I had to *create* small oases of peace for myself. I called one of those oases Sit and Stare Time. Just a few quiet minutes each morning to breathe, to focus on something beautiful. A shaft of sunlight on a coffee cup. The infinite gradients of green in a single geranium leaf. A cat napping with its paw curled over its eyes. Those moments didn't erase the stress, but they steadied me. They reminded me that alongside the difficulty, beauty still existed. Joy still existed. And that I was allowed to feel it.

Joy, after all, doesn't always come easily. Sometimes you have to fight for it. Sometimes you have to choose it, claim it, hold on with both hands while the rest of the world tries to knock it loose. But that fight is worth it. Humor helps me grab hold again. Stillness steadies my grip. Both remind me that joy is never too far away.

Humor and stillness. One loud and rowdy, the other quiet and watchful. Both are ways of fighting for joy when life gets heavy. You don't need to feel joyful all the time to lead a joyful life. You only need to stay open to it—whether that means belly laughter with your children or two minutes of sitting still with your coffee. Allow joy a place at your table, my dear one, however she chooses to show up.

Your Dreams Might Not Look the Same as Everyone Else's

I used to think there was something wrong with me. When all my friends dreamed of exciting lives and huge careers, all I wanted was a pretty, homely life and the simplest kinds of beauty. Once, my teacher asked everyone to draw a picture of what we wanted to be when we grew up. I drew myself surrounded by children, standing next to some bright-flowered curtains I'd sewn, holding a plate of cookies and smiling from ear to ear. "No," she said, "I want to see your job." So I changed the curtains into a blackboard and put desks around the children. "Excellent," she said, her face lighting up, "a teacher!"

I did end up being a teacher—and then a social worker and then an administrator. And yes, there was meaning in those roles. I helped people. I learned things. I gained confidence and skills I never imagined I'd have. But still, deep inside, I longed for something gentler. Something smaller and more rooted. I longed for the kind of life that might not make sense on a resume but made perfect sense in my soul.

It took me a while to achieve my dream of living this quiet, homely life—a home filled with embroidered linens and secondhand treasures, homemade soup simmering on the stove, and the rhythmic comfort of simple routines. But I got here eventually. And oh, how beautiful it is.

Don't worry if your dreams are taking their time to come true. Or if they look different from everyone else's. There is nothing wrong with wanting a life that feels soft and slow. Nothing wrong with dreaming of beauty instead of prestige, of peace instead of applause.

Am I glamorous? No. Am I wealthy or young or slim? No, no, and also no. But am I having fun? Oh, yes. Am I contented and at peace? I am, my darlings. I truly am. I might not have what the world thinks is important, but I have all I need. And I hope, with all my heart, that you have what you need too.

Making Peace with My Pace

One November weekend I set up the porch for winter, just like I always do. I laid out the shelters for the feral cats, filled them with straw, made sure everything was dry and tucked in. I decided to film it: nothing fancy, just me, the porch, the cold air, the rhythm of preparing for what's ahead.

Later, I sat down to watch the video, expecting to see footage of chores getting done. What I saw instead was *me.* I saw my ADHD clear as anything on display in the way I paused mid-task, the way I drifted, the way I started something, half-finished it, wandered off, came back. I could see it so plainly it almost startled me.

For a moment I felt sad. It reminded me of all the times ADHD has made life harder. All the little ways it has tripped me up. But then I looked again, and I saw something else too. I saw how many times I found my way back, how many times I pulled myself together, kept going, got it done. Not neatly, not efficiently, but with persistence, with grit, with tenderness toward myself. Even if I didn't always realize it at the time.

The truth is, my brain doesn't work like most people's. It never has. I am endlessly distractible. I can set out to do something as simple as walk a few laps in the driveway, and suddenly I've forgotten the walk entirely because I've crouched down to admire a patch of lichen or gather little leaves shaped like hearts. I notice things, I forget things. I float through a fog sometimes and land in unexpected places.

For a long time, I thought I had to fix it, that if I tried hard enough, I could change it. But no matter how many planners I bought or routines I attempted to force into place, nothing stuck. Eventually, I stopped trying to be someone I wasn't. I began to work *with* my brain instead of against it. I made space for who I actually am.

And you know what? This odd, unruly mind of mine has helped me survive in ways I didn't even understand until recently. When things were really hard, my brain gave me places to drift to. It gave me beauty. It gave me daydreams when reality was too heavy. It gave me curiosity and a kind of sideways wisdom and the ability to find meaning in small things. It gave me Sit and Stare Time. It even gave me my Internet videos—and it gave me you.

I know I'm not alone in this, and I'm not saying it's easy. Having a mind that works differently is exhausting, especially in a world that rewards efficiency over wonder. So many of us are moving through the world with brains that don't quite fit the mold. Maybe yours is like mine. Maybe you have to work harder than most people realize just to keep up with the basics. Maybe you've built a tool kit, little tricks to help you function: timers, reminders, Post-it notes on mirrors. Maybe it doesn't always work, but you keep trying anyway.

And that effort, that quiet persistence, it matters. It's not invisible, not to me.

I am so proud of you for making it through your days with the brain you have. I know what it takes, I know what it costs, and I know what it gives you too, if you look closely.

It's not easy, but sometimes if you're lucky, your wandering mind will bring you something beautiful along the way.

Thanksgiving in All Its Forms

Holidays have a way of changing, don't they? Over the years, Thanksgiving has looked very different in our house. Once upon a time, the table was long and crowded, full of laughter and clatter and second helpings. There were years when the house was noisy with children and cousins. Years when the oven stayed hot for days and the pie crusts seemed to multiply like rabbits.

But time marches on, and with it, things shift. People move, relationships change, financial realities intervene. The big full Thanksgivings still live in my heart, but so do the quieter ones. Smaller table. Fewer clatters and voices, but still the reverence and love.

One year, my daughter Millen and I had to isolate. Just before Thanksgiving, we'd been exposed to COVID and needed to protect my elderly mother. The house stayed quiet that year, save for the sound of the kettle whistling and our footsteps moving softly through the rooms. Another year, some of my children were living abroad, oceans away, while others stayed away for the holiday due to family conflict. That Thanksgiving was different too. A little heavier, a little lonelier.

And yet each of those Thanksgivings had moments of goodness. There was warm food on the table. There was quiet conversation or a comforting show playing in the background. There was a gentle rhythm of ordinary life continuing, even as the shape of the holiday changed.

I want to gently remind you, my dear, that holidays do change with the seasons of life. Sometimes they're full and bustling, sometimes they're quiet. Sometimes they bring tears. Sometimes, to our great surprise, they bring peace. All of that is okay.

Whether you find yourself gathered in a noisy kitchen bustling with loving family or sitting quietly with your thoughts, know that this day still holds room for beauty. Joy doesn't always arrive with a parade. Sometimes she comes in the hush of a soft morning or the clink of a spoon in your favorite teacup.

Take note of those small, lovely things. Let them count, let them sustain you.

Thank you, truly, for the love you send out into the world. I feel it every day. And I'm sending mine back to you. You are so loved.

You Deserve Rest, Always

Do you get enough rest, my dear?

When we have been busy and active, it's easy to justify taking time out for ourselves, taking time to rest. But on those days when we don't get much of anything done except daydreaming and binge-watching and snacking, when not much of anything goes right and all of our faults and flaws are glaringly obvious, we maybe don't think we deserve rest. We think we need to concentrate, work harder, *get those things done*. But you know what I think? Those lazy, difficult days are when we need rest the most: rest from self-condemnation, rest from pressure, rest from physical activity. Just *rest*.

Maybe when you get up, you'll feel reenergized and able to accomplish All The Things. Maybe you'll be able to accomplish a little bit. But then again, maybe you won't. And that's okay.

We don't need to do anything to deserve rest. We all need rest.

I hope you're taking the rest you need today, my dear. Rest isn't something we earn, no matter how productive (or unproductive!) we have been. Take care of yourself, my dear. Get the rest you need.

Sacred Fragments

Once upon a time, when I was deeply embedded in the evangelical church, I thought I had, if not all the answers, then certainly most of them. I carried those truths around like a well-packed lunch box, always ready to offer something to whoever was hungry. There was a kind of comfort in that certainty, like a well-worn pew or the predictable melody of a hymn. It made me feel helpful, steady, useful.

But when I walked away from the trappings of the evangelical church, I left that self-assurance behind with it. And even though the certainty was misplaced, I sometimes miss it—miss the feeling of always having something to give. Of knowing exactly what to say, even when I probably shouldn't have said it.

What I didn't expect, though, was that in leaving all that behind, my faith wouldn't dissolve, it would deepen. Richer, stranger, freer. The less I clung to structure and certainty, the more clearly I began to see my beloved Jesus. And oh, how brightly He smiled back at me.

The truth is, being part of the conservative evangelical subculture meant that being different was seen as being wrong. It wasn't just about beliefs, it was about conformity. About fitting in. About keeping quiet when something didn't sit right, so you wouldn't be accused of stirring up trouble or, heaven forbid, backsliding! I loved so many of the people there. And I stayed longer than I should have, trying to make myself small enough to fit.

But eventually, I realized something holy: that my different feelings, different prayers, different self were not offenses against God's righteousness. They were expressions of His creativity. The more I accepted myself, the more I felt God's love surround and fill me. The more freedom I felt Him giving to me, the more I knew I had to extend that same freedom to others. What a relief to stop gatekeeping grace.

I've lost confidence in any ironclad version of truth. I've lost the tidy answers and the spiritual shortcuts. But I still have the love. I still have this wide, soft heart that wants to offer shelter and warmth. And maybe that's all the truth any of us really needs.

Because I don't believe that faith was ever meant to be a checklist or a measuring stick. I believe it was meant to be an open door. A meal shared. A laugh between old friends. The warmth of sunlight on your shoulders. I believe God gave us beauty and delight and strangeness on purpose.

And I believe the only thing that truly transforms us is love.

These days, my life might look a bit unconventional. I talk to cats, cry over sunrises, wear vintage aprons, and set my hair in pink sponge rollers. I bake when I'm anxious, sing when I'm happy, and decorate for every single season. I take joy in small things and try to pass that joy along wherever I can.

My faith doesn't come with bullet points anymore. But it's real. It's lived-in. It's honest. And even on the days when I still feel unsure, I rest in this: love is the truest truth I've ever known.

If you're on a winding path too, if your faith looks different now than it used to, or if you're carrying more questions than answers, I want you to know that you're not alone. You're not broken. You're *becoming*. And maybe, just maybe, that old certainty was never the point. Maybe wonder and softness and the courage to love without limits is the holiest thing of all.

Seasons of Change

For years, we rented a sprawling log cabin one weekend each month to gather with my extended family. It had a wraparound porch and overlooked a pond that shimmered with wildlife. Cranes waded in the shallows, fish broke the water's surface with silver flickers, and each spring we watched a pair of ducks return to build their nest. We saw the ducklings hatch, learn to swim, grow strong, and eventually take flight together toward the south. The cycle repeated, year after year.

We celebrated birthdays and anniversaries there. We rocked on that porch through the long golden evenings of summer, watched autumn leaves turn to flame around us, and in the mornings, we stood with coffee cups in hand, dew soaking our shoes as we gazed out at the misty pond.

But the weekend my mother turned ninety, we made the decision to move our monthly gatherings to a smaller, more accessible cottage closer to her home. It was the right decision. Still, that final weekend at the cabin felt sacred. I lingered on the porch, letting the breeze press its soft fingers against my cheek, trying to memorize the sound of wind in the trees and the low murmur of family inside.

This was the last time I'd sit in that rocking chair. The last time I'd sip morning coffee while the ducks glided by. The last time that particular place would be filled with the voices I love.

I've never really liked change. I've gotten better at it, yes, but I still find it hard. Letting go of a place so steeped in memory hurts. It's easy to worry that the new space won't feel the same. That it will lack the comfort and familiarity of what we've known and loved.

But life moves in cycles, doesn't it? The ducks leave, but they come back. The trees go bare, but the leaves return. Familiarity takes time, but it always finds its way back to us.

Instead of focusing on what I was leaving behind, I chose to think about what was ahead: a cozy space that my mother could access easily, new rituals, new memories waiting to be made.

Change is hard. But it helps to remind myself that even the most beloved things were once new and unfamiliar. Even this porch, this view, this tradition, we had to grow into them.

And now it's time to grow into something new.

So as the seasons shift again, and we carry our gatherings into a new space, I do so with gratitude for what has been and hope for what is to come.

Because joy is still ahead. And it's waiting to be found.

Body Gratitude

Last year, I fell down the stairs.

Now don't worry, my dear, nothing was broken, except perhaps my pride, and even that is mostly intact. It was quite a tumble, the kind that feels like it should be set to cartoon music, complete with a flurry of flailing arms and one very startled house cat. But would you believe me if I told you I'm grateful? Truly grateful?

You see, about six years ago, I decided to get up out of my favorite chair, not without a good groan, mind you, and begin what some might generously call "working out." Nothing fancy. A bit of gentle stretching, some walking, a few highly uncoordinated (but hilariously fun!) dance moves in the kitchen. Let's just say I won't be appearing in any fitness advertisements. But I do believe that modest little routine saved me a hospital visit.

When my slippery sock betrayed me on that top step, I somehow had the balance and flexibility to twist in midair like a very surprised cat. A graceless, wide-eyed cat, but a cat nonetheless. And just before I landed—this part makes me laugh—I had the absurd thought, *Well now, this feeling of weightlessness is actually kind of neat*!

Isn't that just nonsense? But I'm grateful for that moment too. For the humor that bubbles up in me even during a pratfall. I'm grateful for the lovely layers of fat that cushioned my old bones. All those generous layers I've sometimes fretted about, tried to shrink, camouflaged under flowing cardigans. Those very curves cushioned my fall. I landed with a thump and a *whoosh* and a very startled yelp, but it wasn't bone that took the brunt. It was softness. The resilient body that's carried me through so much already. *Me.* I'm grateful for years past that taught me how to find light in the dark, how to hold joy in one hand and pain in the other and make friends with them both.

I was a bit tender and rather gorgeously bruised but so grateful.

I wonder, can you find something to be grateful for today? Even if it's just a silly thought as you soar midair or from the comfort of your own feet steady beneath you. Tell me, sweetheart, I'd love to hear it.

On the Art of Letting Go

Decluttering is supposed to feel virtuous, light, clean. But when it comes to pretty things, especially the soft and stitched variety, letting go can feel like being asked to choose your favorite old pet cat and then send them off in a cardboard box labeled "DONATE."

You may think I'm being dramatic, and you would be absolutely correct.

I know I'm not supposed to be so attached to things. I've read the scriptures, done the Bible study intensive. I've been to therapy. I know about minimalism and visual clutter and the psychological freedom of cleared-out drawers. But here's the truth. Sometimes those drawers are full of memory, of comfort, of color and charm in the exact right shade of faded pink that you can never quite find again.

That linen napkin with the frayed edge? It once caught my tears at a very sad dinner and blueberry jam at an incredibly happy breakfast. That chipped little teacup? My daughter held it with both hands when hers were still small enough to disappear inside it. That impossibly tiny apron with the cross-stitched chickens on it? No earthly use, but oh, how it makes me smile!

And so I hesitate. I stall. I stack pretty things into "maybe" piles and then make muffins and think about how pretty the "maybe" piles look sitting there.

But slowly, gratefully—contentedly if I'm lucky—I remind myself things are meant to be used, to be loved, to be shared, not imprisoned in the back of a drawer, hoarded out of fear I'll never find their likes again. And sometimes, the kindest thing you can do for a beloved piece is to set it free. (Thank you, Marie Kondo!) Let it find a second chapter in someone else's story. Let it delight a new kitchen, a new table, a new pair of loving hands.

Letting go of pretty things isn't about not loving them. It's about loving them enough to believe they still have more beauty to give. It's about trusting the Universe or God or yourself enough to believe that you will always have enough—more than enough. Trusting that sharing won't change that. It's about appreciating abundance enough to spread it around.

Of course, this doesn't mean I won't still sniffle a bit when parting with that dish towel with the hand-stitched radishes on it or the potholder that is supposed to be a strawberry but is shaped like a pear and is somehow blue for reasons unknown. (And yes, I've noticed!) But when I send them off, wrapped up in brown paper and tied with string, I do so with the fondest of hopes that someone else will find joy in their faded pinks and soft cottons, that someone else will hang them in their kitchen and feel that little zing of vintage charm that makes the toast taste better and the coffee feel warmer.

And don't worry, I always save lots of pretties for myself. I'm not that noble.

If you too find it difficult to part with pretty things, if you've ever shed a few tears into a linen napkin while folding it neatly into a giveaway box, please know you're not alone. I too love deeply. I too get emotional about gingham and embroidered eggplants. It's not silliness, it's tenderness. And the world needs more of it.

Take your time, let go when you're ready. Until then, stack your maybes, lovingly pour yourself a cup of something warm, and admire the beauty that's passed through your hands.

That's what I'll be doing too.

Gratitude Is a Coping Strategy

Sometimes, when I am in the middle of an especially pleasant little moment, I am struck by this simple realization: I've done nothing to deserve this life. This ease, these beautiful things to wrap myself in. The sunlight slipping through my bedroom window in the early morning. The love and trust of my dearest friends. The warmth and kindness of this wider community.

I have done nothing to earn these things. They are a gift, and I am grateful. Truly, I am so grateful for you, my dear.

I do not always understand why I have been so blessed in this life. There are days when I wrestle with the quiet guilt of it, knowing that so many carry heavy burdens while my arms feel light. It does not always feel fair, and maybe it isn't.

But over the years I have found a way to soften that ache. My coping strategy is simple: gratitude. Gratitude and a promise to pour as much love into the world as I possibly can.

I cannot change the whole world on my own, but I can notice the goodness I have been given. I can share it. I can let my life be shaped by thankfulness and by kindness.

And for now, for today, I think that might be enough.

Permission Slips for the Soul

(torn from the pages of someone who finally gave herself a little grace)

Tucked in the lining of every perfectly odd life are tiny, invisible notes: little permission slips you forgot to write yourself. So here, my darling. Let's write them now.

You have permission . . .

To say no without explaining.

To say yes with your whole heart.

To cry in public and laugh too loud and not feel the need to apologize for either.

To wear the thing that makes you happy, even if it's not "flattering."

To not care what "flattering" means.

To leave a party early.

To skip the party entirely.

To throw a party of your own that only includes tea, your cat, and a 1940s record you found for fifty cents.

You have permission to change your mind.

To change your name.

To change your rhythm, your path, your pace.
To go slowly. To go softly. To go strangely.

You have permission to be happy, even when other people aren't.
To be okay, even when the world is not.
To protect your peace like a precious heirloom and hand it out only when it feels safe to do so.

You have permission to love what you love.
To collect what you collect.
To get giddy over vintage buttons or outdated cookbooks or moth-eaten quilts with names stitched into the corners.

You have permission to believe that joy counts—even small joy, especially small joy.
The kind that flutters by on an ordinary Tuesday and lands in your hair like confetti.

And most of all?

You have permission to be exactly who you are, without shrinking, without smoothing the edges, without rehearsing your lines first.

Print these out if you need to. Tuck them into your purse.
Write them in lipstick on your mirror.
Text them to a friend who needs one.
Fold them into a tiny square and keep them in your pocket, right next to your odd little treasures and lint and that Happy Trap piece of candy.

This world is better with your particular glow in it.
Shine, darling. Shine just as you are.

Winter

Winter quiets the world. Snow hushes the landscape, evenings lengthen, and even our hearts feel slower, more contemplative. Here is the season of tucking in, of reflecting on what has been lost and what has been found. Of reframing failure, mourning with honesty, and cherishing small lights against the long dark. Winter invites us to rest, to listen, to discover the beauty that can only be seen in stillness.

In the Season of Winter

Long past are those lazy summer evenings
on the front porch,
eating ice cream,
chatting with passing neighbors,
watching the kids play in the street
until it gets dark.
Winter evenings are different.
They're shorter
and quieter
and colder.
We don't have the neighbors
or their children,
but we do have each other.
We have warm sweaters
and we have old television shows to watch.
We have new books to read.
We have the time
to make an event
out of our evening cup
of Sleepytime tea.
Different seasons
bring different things
into our lives.

If we spend our evenings
missing the ice cream,
we never really get
to enjoy the tea.

Enjoy the season
you're in right now,
my dear.
Even if it feels
cold and dark,
there's always something
that's warm
and cozy.
And bright sunny days
will come back
in their time.

What's Wrong with Being Old?

"You should dress a little younger. After all, you're not *that* old!"

It's a comment I hear more often than you'd think: on videos, in messages, sometimes even in person. And here's the thing: I take no offense. I know it's kindly meant. But it always makes me chuckle because I have a few thoughts in response.

First, I'm not dressing *old.* I'm dressing *vintage.* I dress the way a woman in her forties or fifties or sixties might have dressed in the 1940s or '50s. There's an elegance and dignity to that era that still sings to me: a little structured, a little whimsical, always charming.

Second, well, I *am* old. Not ancient, mind you, but I was born in the mid-1950s, so I've earned my stripes. And honestly? I wouldn't trade places with my younger self for anything. This might be the oldest I've ever been, but it's also the happiest I've ever been. This season of life, wrinkles and back aches and all, is rich with joy.

We're taught to fear aging, to resist it at every turn. But age is not a failure. It's not something to dodge or disguise. It's a gift. It's experience, perspective, growth. It's knowing what matters and what doesn't, what to fret over and what to let go.

And the older I get, the more I realize that I don't want to spend my precious time trying to be anything other than what I am. I'm not here to trick anyone into thinking I'm younger or sleeker or trendier than I am. I'm here to be me. Fully, joyfully, sincerely me.

For the Odd Ones

Sometimes I like to imagine that I'm a courageous little old lady from a storybook, braving the freezing blizzard, risking my life to gather the medicinal herbs that will save all the town's people from a dreadful epidemic. Sometimes I'm just chubby little old me, traipsing across my snowy driveway to clip greens for my floral arrangements. And the only thing I'm risking is cold feet. But I'll tell you what—either way, I'm having fun.

Do people ever think you're a bit odd? Disapprove of your choices?

Me too, my friend, me too. And often about the silliest things.

For years, folks told me that my hairstyle made me look too old. They thought I should wear it down or try a different updo or cut it short altogether. But the truth is, I love my hair. I love the way I wear it. It brings me joy. I don't need anyone else to approve of it. It feels like me, and that is reason enough to hold on to my choice.

I remember my very first popular video shared on social media. It was just me styling my hair. I didn't expect much from it. I certainly didn't think anyone would care. But something about it resonated. I was so shocked by the response. Yes, some folks criticized my hairstyle, some folks laughed and thought it made me look "too old." But mostly folks were wonderful. Since then, so many kind people have reached out, offered encouragement, and shared their warmth. Over time, this little corner of the Internet has grown into a community. Full of connection and kindness, and that has changed my life. Truly. I'm so grateful.

So let me say this to you: Don't let the disapproval or disdain of others keep you from doing what gives you joy. Yes, some folks might exclude you. Some might whisper, roll their eyes, or decide you are not their kind, but others will see you and fall in love.

Your people will find you and not just tolerate you but be inspired by you: by unusual, beautiful, odd, courageous you.

So, carry on, exactly as you are. The right hearts will know you when they see you.

My Least Favorite Chore

Sometimes we don't need a change of circumstance, we just need a change of focus.

Brushing the snow off my car is one of my very least favorite things to do. But if I shift my focus from the cold to the bright freshness of the air, from the difficulty of reaching the tippy top of my car to the good feeling of stretching my muscles, from the nuisance of the snow to the beauty of the snow, it's really not so bad. Not bad at all.

Your Best Is Good Enough

Every year around the winter holidays, I start to feel a little bit disappointed in myself.

It always sneaks up on me. I begin with beautiful plans, ideas full of sparkle and scent and reminiscence, but before long I find myself quietly comparing the grandeur of the holiday I imagined with the reality of the one I'm actually living.

Maybe the craft projects I planned aren't quite as fun or as lovely as I had hoped. Maybe I've resorted to using a box mix for the Christmas muffins I usually make from scratch. There's always a gift or two that still hasn't arrived in the mail, with no sign of when it might come. And somehow, I never manage to get all of my holiday baking done in time.

There's always so much to do. Gifts, decoration, performances, religious services, parties, baking. It can feel never-ending. Honestly, it can be so much pressure.

I know I'm not alone in this. The holidays can bring out our most ambitious selves. There's a kind of energy that comes from imagining something elaborate, something perfect, something memorable. And there's nothing wrong with dreaming that way. Those gorgeous, ambitious plans can feel exciting and full of possibility.

But when those plans begin to weigh on us, when our own high expectations turn into quiet self-criticism, when perfectionism slips in and makes us feel like we've fallen short, it's time to let them go. Every year I have to remind myself of this. I have to relax my expectations. I have to pause and remember that my best, even if it looks simpler, quieter, or a little bit messier than I had imagined, is still good enough.

And I want to remind you of that too.

Whatever your best looks like right now, let it be enough—whether you manage to carefully unpack each and every ornament, hang every strand of lights, and fill your home with the scent of cinnamon and cloves, or you simply fall asleep watching *It's a Wonderful Life* with a cat on your lap. However you show up for the season, for your loved ones, for yourself, let it count. You are already enough.

Needing Help Isn't a Failing

Over the years, I've gotten older, as we all do. I've gotten weaker in my physical body, a bit too accustomed to the comforts of home (some might say). More settled in. Less daring . . . not that I've ever been particularly adventurous! I've always needed help, especially with big things. But these days I need a gentle on-ramp. I need hand-holding and encouragement and time to rest afterward. For a long while, I saw that as a flaw. I felt guilty for needing support, embarrassed that I couldn't just power through the way some folks do.

But wishing myself to be someone different never made me different. It only made me tired. The only thing that has ever helped me grow stronger is kindness. Kindness to myself. Acceptance of who I am and how I operate.

These days, I try not to fight so hard against my nature. I accept that I need softness. I welcome the support that helps me shine. I let my best be enough. That gets easier with age too.

So no, I'm not dressing younger. I'm dressing like me. I'm not hiding my age—I'm living it out loud. And while I may not be glamorous or wealthy or particularly important in the worldly sense, I am deeply happy.

And I hope, my dear one, that you are learning to be gentle with yourself too. That you accept your needs, your pace, your quirks. That you let your best be enough. Because it is. It always has been.

And remember, there is nothing wrong with being old. Especially when you get to do it *your* way.

Hard-Day Jeans

When the whole world feels chaotic, our own inner world can feel chaotic as well. It can be hard to maintain one's peace. Outside our wintry windows, we might see glittering snowflakes drifting gently out of a blue-gray sky, colorful birds contentedly nibbling away at feeders, holiday lights glinting and glowing from our dear neighbors' homes, but somehow, inside we are unable to be at rest. Joy can feel impossible, especially when others are suffering. Focusing on our own peace of mind feels selfish. Our own joy seems trivial. But, my dear one, there is nothing more important in difficult times. Inner peace strengthens us. Your joy strengthens others, especially when you refuse to give in to despair, when you allow yourself to experience silly, frivolous joy. When you grasp onto hope, when you stubbornly hold it tight with both hands and refuse to let it go, your hope spreads to others—first one, then another—and then their hope reaches still more hopeless ones, all because of you.

Be strong, little one: you're changing the world.

Lately when I'm struggling, I reach for my *hard day jeans*. It's a battered old pair with patches and embroidery, visible mending cradling soft, worn denim. One knee is covered by a scrap of a 1930s feed sack quilt. The back pockets each boast a small potholder with a cat face lovingly stitched by hand, each with a little old red plastic button at the top, for absolutely no reason whatsoever except cuteness. There's even a patch from when I was in high school in the 1970s that says Make Peace, Not War.

And on the hardest days, I don't try to fix everything. I simply add one more patch. I take my time choosing just the right fabric or button, something small and pretty. I sit in a sunbeam on my cozy chair with my needle and thread, and I mend. Mending keeps my hands busy. I turn off my phone, which slows my racing thoughts, quiets the overwhelm. And when I finish even one tiny thing—a stitch, a seam, a square—I feel just a bit steadier, like maybe I can handle the rest of what's weighing on me.

The jeans may never be finished, but being done is not the point. They are a project that is always waiting, welcoming, and ready to meet me exactly where I am.

Often as I stitch, one of my cats hops up beside me and bats at the thread. He'll flop onto the denim, look up at me with wide eyes, and ask without a sound to be noticed. And I pause, because there's no task more important than giving love to those who need it. The thread can wait. The mending can wait. But loving someone in the moment they ask for it? That is sacred work.

So I pause the stitching. I run my fingers through my cat's fur. I whisper sweet things, and in that moment, the world softens.

Let yourself mend, darling, and let yourself be mended. Rest, stitch, love, begin again. You're not alone.

The Candle Cupboard

I used to be really into New Year's resolutions. The holidays gave me plenty of time to reflect upon my flaws and inadequacies, and in the rosy flush of New Year's morning, I would determine that *this* was going to be the year I finally overcame at least some of them. Diets, fitness plans, budgets, professional goals all organized in a spreadsheet were the order of those days. Day-by-day housecleaning systems, meal-planning journals! Brand-new homeschool curriculum! (Never mind that January 1 is the exact middle of the school year!) But of course, expecting copious amounts of self-discipline to magically appear simply because we've arrived at a date on a calendar rarely works . . . correction: it never works. At least it never did for me.

Somewhere along the way, that drive to set and chase New Year's resolutions fell by the wayside. Not because I gave up on myself but because I learned to know myself better. Rigid rules and stern ultimatums have never suited me. They paralyze me and fill me with dread. There's a rebellious little part of me that resists rules, even when I've made those rules myself. Gentle works better for me. *Gradually* is the way I change. Instead of thinking of the New Year as a time to crack the whip on myself, I like to think of each New Year as a pleasant invitation, an open door to ease into a few small nourishing habits that might, just might, make life a little brighter.

This year, one of those new habits is simple. Each week I choose one space in my home—a drawer, a cupboard, a closet, even the back porch—and give it a little attention. I set it to rights, nothing grand or overwhelming. I am not implementing a radical new home organization scheme. I'm just trying a quiet rhythm of bringing order to one small corner at a time.

The first space I tackled was my little candle cupboard in the sideboard in my dining room. What a sight it was! As I cautiously lifted the latch, I could hear jars and boxes shifting within the cupboard. They leaned against the door as I opened it. Loose matches spilled out. Errant half-burned birthday candles escaped and gleefully rolled across the floor. The cupboard was crammed: tall jar candles teetering precariously, half-empty boxes of tea lights, mismatched warmers, loose wicks, and boxes of wooden matches. There were wax melts stacked haphazardly behind everything else, long-forgotten votives rolling loose in the corners. Every candle-related supply you can imagine had somehow found its way into that one crowded space.

As I pulled everything out and spread it across the dining room table, it quickly became obvious how much of it I could let go. The tea lights with no matching holders, the half-melted candles I was never going to burn, the wicks that had become brittle with age. Out they went! I released them without guilt, making room for what I loved and wanted to use.

Next came the sorting. I tucked everything into clear-lidded stackable containers, each one carefully labeled: scented candles, beeswax, tea lights, matches, warmers, wax melts. And then the most satisfying part: I placed it all back into the cupboard. Everything fit with room to spare. Now when I open that little door, I can see at a glance exactly what I need.

No more rummaging and digging. No more frustrated hunts for that box of matches buried in the back.

There's a quiet kind of power in bringing order to disorder. It's not about perfection, it's about breathing fresh life into a tired space. Giving your belongings the dignity of their proper place. In some small way, it feels like offering a bit of dignity to myself as well.

Because life can be like that candle cupboard, can't it? We gather memories, commitments, responsibilities, until we find ourselves overwhelmed by the sheer weight of it all. But when we pause, take things gently in hand, we can release what no longer serves us. When we put the rest into order, we make space to breathe again. We make space for light to shine.

One little cupboard at a time, my dearest, that's all it takes.

For When the World Feels a Bit Too Loud

Sometimes when I am feeling anxious, I step away from my racing mind for just a minute. Nothing dramatic. Just a quiet pause.

I look around for something small that makes me smile . . . like kitty footprints in the snow.

I listen for a pleasant sound . . . the *crunch crunch* of my boots through the ice, maybe.

I reach out and move something gently with my hands . . . brushing snow from a branch, feeling the texture.

I breathe in . . . pine, maybe. Or winter air, crisp and bright.

I let myself notice the beauty.

Then I think of something I'm grateful for. Just one thing.

It helps.

It really helps.

Maybe it will help you too?

The Hair I Lost, the Strength I Found

I was losing my hair.

I noticed a thinning at first, easy to dismiss under soft lighting and wishful thinking, but then the strands came loose by the handful each time I shampooed. It stopped being subtle. It stopped being something I could ignore.

It was likely a side effect of a blood pressure medication I was taking at the time mixed in with a few ill-advised hair care experiments. (Pro tip, darlings, never use straight white vinegar as a setting lotion, no matter how charmingly old-fashioned it sounds.) Whatever the reason, I lost about three-quarters of my hair. And I'll be honest with you, I didn't take it very well.

My vanity took a hit. I was scared. I grieved the thick, shiny hair that had always felt like such a defining part of me. And there was no neat resolution, no quick fix, just questions and the uncomfortable possibility that this might be my new normal.

In that fragile season, I learned something important. Sometimes we lose beautiful things. Sometimes we are forced into new versions of ourselves we didn't ask for, and no matter how much we cry or protest, there's not a single thing we can do to rewind time and undo the loss.

Because darling,
we don't only deserve
comfort when we are
shining and confident.
We deserve comfort when
we feel scraggly and
strange and half undone.

So I let myself grieve. I cried all the tears. I wore soft hats, and I bought silk pillow cases for comfort. I avoided mirrors on hard days. And slowly, I also let myself reach for joy. I watched my favorite shows, ate chocolate while wrapped up cozy in warm quilts, and accepted every single kind word that came my way.

Because darling, we don't only deserve comfort when we are shining and confident. We deserve comfort when we feel scraggly and strange and half undone.

The good news is I have new growth now, and while it doesn't quite resemble the thick curtain of hair I once had, it is mine. It is growing, it is healthy, and it is full of promise. I still don't know exactly how things will turn out. Maybe my hair will never be what it was. Maybe it will surprise me and grow even better than before. But you know what? Either way, I will be okay. I will be *more* than okay.

Because through it all, I've learned that our strength isn't in having things turn out perfectly. It's in continuing to love ourselves through the messy middle. And choosing joy even when it feels silly or hard.

Let yourself grieve, my dear one. But don't forget to let yourself laugh too. Let yourself hope. You've survived every single thing this world has brought you so far, and you will survive this too. And maybe, just maybe, your resilience, your brave, silly hope, your joy will light the way for someone else who needs it too.

Learning to Move

I'm going to tell you something about myself that may come as no surprise whatsoever. I loathe exercising. I really do. But my dear ones, I've learned something over the years. Often, the thing I least want to do is exactly what I most need.

When I'm struggling, all I want to do is curl up and hide away, isolate, pull the blankets over my head, shut off my phone, and tell myself I'm resting. That I will start my new workout plan tomorrow or call to set up that follow-up appointment later. But I've learned there's a difference between curling up in genuine rest and curling up in retreat. Rest restores. Hiding erodes. Rest is a kindness. Hiding . . . well, hiding is like eating frosting straight from the mixing bowl: it feels good in the moment but leaves you worse off in the end.

Recently, when I was feeling especially low, close to tears all day, I did something that felt hard. I reached out to a dear old friend and we sat together and talked for hours. And it helped more than I can say.

That same week, I forced myself to go to a doctor's appointment I'd been avoiding. I listened to some hard things he had to tell me. And then I found a workout class designed for chubby little old ladies like me, even though the thought of being in a gym makes me cringe. I cleared the clutter off my front porch, swept away winter's remains, and brought out two little chairs. Now I sit out there in the mornings with my coffee, feeling the breeze and watching the birds. It's peaceful, it's healing. But none of it came easily.

You see, real self-care isn't all bubble baths and chocolate cake. It isn't self-indulgence. It's not doing-whatever-feels-good self-care. True self-care often asks us to do the unfun thing, the one that takes effort, the one we'd rather not do. It asks us to move our bodies when we're tired, to speak to someone when we feel like retreating, to tidy a corner of our home so we can breathe a little more freely.

Early in the morning, even though my heart may be heavy and my body sluggish, I make myself take one of my little walks around the driveway. And wouldn't you know, after just a few laps, the clouds in my chest begin to lift. The fresh air, the birdsong, the rhythm of my steps: all of it came together to remind me that I'm still here, still trying, still caring for myself in the quietest, hardest of ways.

Today, my darling, ask yourself what you really need, not what feels easiest. Not what seems most comforting in the moment but what will care for the soft animal of your body and the tender spirit inside it. You deserve a life filled with the things you love, and sometimes to get there, you have to begin with the things you most definitely do not love.

The life you long for is built on tiny, brave choices. So go ahead and take that first small step. I promise it matters more than you know.

The Not-Perfect Tree

When I ordered this little artificial Christmas tree, I was sure it would be absolutely perfect. Slim and tidy, just the right height, a bargain at $25. I pictured it glowing in front of our big front windows, looking magazine-worthy and magical.

But when it arrived, oh gracious. It was . . . not perfect.

It was so narrow it looked like it had been starved. The poor thing had about four branches and all the festive spirit of a coatrack. I hauled it from room to room, trying to find its best angle like a hopeful stylist with an uncooperative model. I tried it in front of the windows. I tried it in the corner. I even tried it in the kitchen. But no matter where I placed it, it just looked sad.

And the worst part? I could see it from nearly every room in our tiny house. My $25 bargain mocked me from all directions.

For a few days, I let myself stew in the irritation. But eventually, because stewing gets tiresome, I took a breath and made peace with it. I didn't have the funds for a new tree, but I could change the way I decorated this one. We made some new ornaments, shifted around the old ones, and with a bit of rearranging, something began to change. Not the tree, really—but my heart.

Life is just full of disappointments, my dear. Scrawny Christmas trees, dream jobs that turn into an unbearable grind, strained friendships, failed marriages. And while we usually aren't able to make huge changes and make everything better, often we can make small changes, and often even small changes can make things better. So much better. They can give us back our joy.

And sometimes, that's enough. More than enough. Even now, I think of that ridiculous little tree with more fondness than I ever expected. It wasn't perfect—but it turned out just fine.

Beautiful, Used, and Deeply Loved

I have altogether too many kitchen linens.

Old tablecloths, napkins, dishcloths, funny little coaster sets. Sweet handmade potholders with cat faces embroidered on them and those charming, endearingly childish days-of-the-week dish towels. I've lost count of how many full sets I own. I just love them all. I love the old graphics of fruit or anthropomorphic vegetables. I am drawn to the handmade quality of the finishes and the colors, brights and pastels, jewel tones and neutrals, all blended together in the same piece. Somehow, everything harmonizes. Somehow, none of it clashes. Despite my best efforts, it's almost impossible for me to say no to acquiring just one or two or seven more.

In my dining room sits a lovely old pine server with deep drawers all across the front. Every single one of those drawers is full of kitchen linens, neatly sorted by category: napkins, tablecloths, and sets. And it doesn't stop there. I have baskets of linens. I have boxes of linens. The special dish towel sets are in the upstairs linen cupboard. Out-of-season table linens are in a cheap little chest at the very back of the front hall coat closet. There may even be a few tucked in with the board games.

People often ask if I actually use my vintage things or if they're just for display. Although I do keep a few pristine pieces tucked away like precious little museum artifacts, most of my beloved old things are in regular, joyful use. My 1930s Dripolator coffee maker with its cheery red apple painted on the side brews my coffee every morning. My translucent green jadeite dishes hold toast and jam. I still haul my battered old copper watering can around the yard every morning—dripping slightly, just like it surely did in the 1940s. None of these things are particularly valuable in a monetary sense. The Bakelite comb I treasure is missing a tooth. My white cashmere sweater, made long before I was born, has a stain or two, but I can usually hide them with a brooch. My beloved chenille bedspread has lost several bobbles over the years, but her worn spots keep me from fretting too much when the cats conduct their daily acrobatics atop it. And my favorite creamy silk scarf? The hem is forever in need of repair. She's frayed, but those frays don't show when she's tucked neatly into the neckline of an old rayon dress. Because here's the funny thing: I don't mind the flaws.

I used to. I used to think lovely things needed to be pristine to be worthy. I used to worry what others would think if my tablecloth was almost worn through, if my dish had a chip, if my sweater had a stain. But now I find imperfections so freeing. A missing bobble, a chipped saucer, a wobbly stitch. They all let me off the hook. They remind me that nothing has to be perfect to be meaningful or beautiful.

Some things we love, we're lucky enough to keep for a lifetime. But most things, no matter how dear, are with us only for a season. That's just the way life works. So I try not to hoard beauty. I don't want to tuck it away and protect it so fiercely that it never gets to do its job: to be seen, or used, or to give joy. Every so often, I go through those deep drawers, those baskets and boxes, and sort through my treasures. I pass some along to friends who love them too. It's never easy. I won't pretend otherwise. Letting go of beloved things is hard. But I've learned to be humble enough to know that someone else might love them more. Might care for them better than I, might give them a second or third life. And I try to be trusting enough to believe that my hands, once emptied, will be filled with new loveliness in time.

Because at the heart of it all, here's what I've learned: Things don't have to be perfect to be beautiful. And they certainly don't have to be perfect to be loved.

Even When I Disappoint Myself

Some days, my darling, I am confronted by the reality of my own failures, and oh my, those times can be hard. There was that time I completely flubbed a presentation at work and missed a deadline. Or when I forgot to sign that field trip permission form, forgot my dear friend's birthday, bought that silly thing on credit. I didn't meet the mark I'd set. I dropped a ball I meant to carry, and I disappointed someone else. But most painfully, I disappointed me.

It stings, doesn't it? That quiet oh-so-personal embarrassment or heartbreak. There's a moment sometimes (or often) when all I can see are the ways I failed. I notice the dust I didn't sweep, the words I didn't say, the promise I didn't keep. I dwell there for a moment, sometimes longer than I should, and I begin to believe the lie that my failings define me.

But here's what I know to be true. Failing at one thing does not mean I failed at everything. A moment's misstep doesn't erase the miles I've walked with care and courage. My darlings, failure might just be a roundabout way to get to your destination..

So when I find myself in that tender, disappointed place, I still give myself the gifts of beauty and joy. I give myself pleasant little tasks to do. Folding a soft towel, trimming the edge of a wandering plant. I wash all those lovely little vintage hankies, and then hang them out in the sun to dry, fresh and bright and clean. I take the time to notice pleasant, lovely things. I remind myself of my successes: *I am still good. I am still me. I am still safe.*

You are too, my dear. Even on your worst day, you carry within you the same kind and hopeful heart, the same gifts, the same precious light you had on your best. Your value has not diminished because things didn't go as planned.

Beauty Waits Quietly

Not every day is bright and happy, my dear. Some days are wintry and dark. We have times of grief, times when our heart breaks, days when we finally, finally realize that our dream won't be coming true, and we start to learn to live without that thing we have been so longing for. Some days are just full of annoyances and try our patience. But even on our very worst days, there's also joy and beauty and humor, amusement and love. They can coexist like two currents in a river. Pain insists we pay attention to her while beauty waits quietly until we notice her. Joy waits until we call her in. But that doesn't mean that heartache is more important than joy. Sadness doesn't make beauty less beautiful. In the midst of your hardest days, look for beauty. Invite joy to keep you company. Cultivate their companionship, my dear, and they will become your closest friends.

A Lesson in Humility

(stitched with love)

I've always wanted to sew myself a wardrobe of dreamy 1940s dresses, nipped waists, swishy full skirts—all the charm of another era. I've always prided myself on my nifty garment construction skills, thank you very much. I know my way around a French seam, I can install a zipper without throwing anything across the room (most of the time), and my buttonholes are downright respectable.

But the truth is, I've never quite mastered how to make those lovely dresses fit *me*. Not really. I've always skipped over the fitting step, assuming I could eyeball it. Turns out, I can't.

So this year, I did something that made me feel a little foolish and a lot brave: I bought a beginner's book on fitting. The kind with diagrams and simple language and no assumption that you've sewn a single thing before. And as I flipped through its pages, something in me relaxed.

Sometimes the thing keeping us from reaching our goals isn't a lack of talent or time, it's pride. It's the quiet little voice saying, *You should already know how to do this.* But here's the secret: Being a lifelong learner means being willing to be a beginner. Again and again.

Humility isn't weakness. It's a doorway. And walking through it might just be the thing that helps you finally stitch the life (or dress) you've been dreaming of.

Just Throw the Axe

You'll never guess what I tried doing. What's the most un-chubby-vintage-Nana thing you can think of? Did you guess: going to an axe-throwing bar and trying my hand at hurling sharp objects? Yes? Because that's exactly what I did. I went in with enthusiasm and optimism, and wearing a cardigan. And my dears, I was *terrible* at it.

I threw that axe and threw it again. Tried every stance, every tip from the helpful young man wearing flannel, who could've been my grandson. I adjusted my grip. I focused. I breathed deeply. And still, not once did that axe stick in the target. Not once.

Was I embarrassed? A bit. Mostly because I thought I'd be better at it. I thought I'd be one of those surprising older ladies who just casually nails it on her first try. (Spoiler alert: I wasn't.) Did I secretly envision the entire bar erupting into surprised applause at my impressive axe- throwing talent? *Maybe.* (Spoiler alert: they didn't.) But was my time wasted? Not one bit.

Because the trying is the point. The showing up, the laughing at yourself, the learning. The willingness to look silly. To fail. To still have fun anyway. To not let fear of imperfection keep you from stepping up to the line.

Sometimes you try something and the axe lands with a satisfying thwack. Sometimes it clatters to the floor. But either way, you've stretched yourself. You've risked looking ridiculous. And that, my dear, is a quiet kind of bravery.

Success and failure are not opposites. They often hold hands. They often share the same story.

So go ahead. Try the thing. Even if you're bad at it. Especially if you're bad at it. You're learning. You're growing. And that matters more than any bullseye ever could.

Rest Before Your Important Work

It's easy to feel helpless when the world feels like it's spinning too fast. When the headlines make your heart race and your chest ache. When cruelty is loud and compassion seems too quiet. It's easy to feel like we ought to be doing more, saying more, showing up for every cause and every crisis with unwavering energy and perfect words. It can feel wrong to take a break, wrong to rest.

But my dear one, rest is not an escape from the work that matters. It is how we make that work possible.

In times like these, the kindest thing you can do for yourself and your work is to slow down. Tuck yourself into your coziest corners. Surround yourself with those who truly know you, who trust your heart, and whose hearts you trust too. Do what makes your body feel at ease. Pull on your softest sweater. Sip something warm, eat something nourishing. Read a book you already know by heart. Let the rhythm of your breathing come back to itself.

Use your hands, your eyes, your imagination. Stitch something together, bake something warm. Paint a small corner of your world in color. Not because it will solve the world's problems but because it might strengthen your spirit. To keep going, let beauty, creativity, and rest refuel you. Let them remind you that gentleness is not frivolous. It is powerful. It is sacred.

If the world feels like too much today, I hope you'll let yourself pull away for a bit. You don't need to be everywhere all at once. You don't need to carry it all. You just need to be well enough to do *your* part in *your* way when the time is right. And in the meantime, I hope you'll treat yourself with the same tenderness you offer everyone else.

You are important, your work is important, but your well-being is what makes that work sustainable.

Rest, dear one, refuel, and come back when you're ready, with love still beating strong in your heart.

Some Days Are Small

Some days are huge and glittering and filled with outsized happiness. Weddings, that well-deserved promotion, the day that long-separated family members are reunited at last. We often think that Christmas *should* be like that: huge and happy and bursting with outsized everything. We see visions of holiday perfection everywhere and, without even thinking it through, we put pressure on ourselves to match (or exceed!) those gloriously extravagant celebrations. Like there's something wrong when Christmas is small. But you know, some days are small. Some Christmases are small and quiet and gentle and beautiful. Christmas doesn't need to be the same from year to year, my dear, or from house to house.

One year, we were planning on a big family Christmas in a beautiful, sprawling, old log cabin down by my mother's house. Millen had parties to go to and lots of gifts to give and receive. But at the last minute, we discovered that we'd been exposed to COVID, and we ended up at home instead. This was during the height of the pandemic, that year that so many millions of us were forced to quiet our expectations, to make smaller choices to help keep everyone safe. Instead of the noise and bustle and delicious chaos of a cabin full of family, it was just Millen and me at home, in our tiny cottage. We had just a single stocking hanging by the fireplace. Just a few small gifts beneath our little tabletop tree. We didn't have roast turkey and ham and dozens of side dishes, but we had a little roast chicken with stuffing, homemade cranberry sauce simmering quietly on the back burner, tiny baked jacket potatoes with just a bit of gravy, plus microwaved veggies and a pie made of blueberries from the depths of the freezer. We had time, hours spreading out before us with nowhere to go and no one to see. And they were such pleasant hours spent together. We had candy canes in our evening cocoa. We had an early bedtime and hours of restful sleep. That quiet "alone" Christmas seemed like a catastrophe at first, but it ended up being one of our best Christmases ever.

No matter what your holidays look like, no matter how big or small your celebrations are this year, I wish you beauty and peace and joy.

The Simple Things Are Plenty

One year I ordered a teeny little Christmas tree through our local grocery store. It was sweet and tiny, fresh and pretty and bright. It fit just right into my old vintage Christmas tree stand. It fit just right into my little house. It fit just right into my little vintage budget.

So often during the holidays we are tempted to overspend. We see the grand decorations and the piles of gifts and the expensive holiday foods and, in comparison, our quiet little celebrations, our old decorations, our homemade everything can start to feel like they aren't quite enough.

But you and I both know that things do not have to be big or showy or expensive to be beautiful, my dear.

The battered old ornaments, crafted and glued by tiny hands, are more precious than anything new or trendy. Paper chains, cranberry garlands, cut-out snowflakes . . . do those ever really go out of style? Even the simple, inexpensive things are lovely at Christmas. The plain old things still bring joy.

The simple things are plenty. The simple things are more than enough.

There is no shame in having a limited budget, my dears. Having lots of money to spend on gifts and celebrations is wonderful fun, but having less money does not make you less worthy or less capable of creating beauty.

In fact, you can be proud. Proud of your self-discipline when you resist the pull to overspend. Proud of your creativity when you are able to make much out of little.

And I am proud of you too.

January Reflections

Every January ushers in the same rhythm. The holidays are over, and it will be time to move back into everyday life again. And as much as I love filling every corner of my home with festive Christmas loveliness, I love putting it all away every bit as much. The flashing lights and brightly wrapped days of December give way to the long, gray days of January. Holiday obligations and pressures give way to solitude and quiet hours of simple work. The January plainness of my home feels orderly and peaceful.

When we are in the middle of an exciting phase of life, like the energizing bounty of summer, it feels like the best of times. Quieter, more ordinary days feel dull in comparison. But they have their beauty too. And if we let it, that beauty will give us the strength to face whatever changes lie ahead.

Honestly, January might be my favorite month. It is a month of quiet rest and beauty that sets the stage or establishes a baseline for the new, fresh year to come.

I never really suffer from the post-holiday letdown because I'm going to tell you a secret: The week between Christmas and New Year is my very favorite week of the whole year. My house is still sparkling with little touches of holiday cheer. Fairy lights tucked under the porch eaves, a string of holiday cards fluttering cheerfully in the window. The refrigerator is bursting with delicious leftovers, cheesecake, pumpkin pie, cookies, boxes and boxes of chocolate. The big meals have been served. The presents are unwrapped, and the obligations have quieted. My family is nearby, my home is clean, and the calendar holds no demands.

So when I find myself enjoying my second cup of coffee on a serene January morning, I'll think of you. I'm wishing you sweetness and softness. Wishing you Sit and Stare Time. Wishing you rest.

As much as I adore the glitter and bustle of the holidays, the end of them feels refreshing. A lull, a blessing, a chance to clear the decks. Wipe the counters, fold the linens, and quietly start again.

Mama Cat Memorial

Her name was Mama Cat.

She wasn't my cat—not technically. She belonged to no one. A weathered, wiry little scrap of a thing, with patchy fur and narrowed eyes, she'd spent most of her life just barely surviving. She'd show up on my porch every single day, squinting at me like she wasn't sure if I was friend or foe. And for a long time, I wasn't sure either.

She was mean, if I'm honest. Not in a fun, feisty way, but just plain ornery. She swiped at the other cats. She growled at any kindness. She hissed when I left food and spat when I tried to offer more. But still, I kept feeding her. I couldn't not. I'm not a cat lover so much as I'm a suffering-hater. And oh, how she had suffered.

Her body told the story: scarred, thin, exhausted. She'd had so many litters of kittens—far too many for her fragile frame. Most of them vanished, one by one, because honestly, she was even mean to her own babies. But still, she kept surviving. Still, she kept coming back.

Eventually, after years of failed attempts, we trapped her. Got her spayed. Vaccinated. Safe.

And wouldn't you know, she changed. We'd hoped her health would improve. We'd dreamed of her life growing a little easier. But what happened next was more than we ever dared imagine. The transformation wasn't just real—it was radiant. Wonderfully, startlingly so. She softened. She stopped fighting. She'd sit quietly in the corner of the porch, soaking in the sunlight. Her fur grew in thick and sleek. She gained weight. Her eyes seemed brighter. Her whole spirit shifted. And oh, the joy we felt to see such a distressed creature finally, finally at rest.

When she was hit by a car, I almost convinced myself not to care. She wasn't really mine, after all. But that night I curled up with a comfort dinner of macaroni and cheese, streamed old murder mysteries, and sobbed. And the next day, we wrapped her tiny body and brought her to a beautiful farm. We buried her by a corner of the barn, near a stream of cool, clear water. A year later, my son-in-law brought me scarlet roses from her grave that bloomed, unexpectedly, above her resting place.

I placed them in a chipped vintage pitcher on my dining room table. They reminded me that you don't have to own something to love it. A being doesn't have to be lovable to be worthy. She wasn't easy. She wasn't gentle. But she was loved.

And oh, how much she taught me.

She taught me that love can come quietly, grudgingly, over time. That healing is possible, even after years of pain. That comfort and safety can soften the sharpest edges.

This summer, new cats will come to my porch. Some wild, some starving for food, some starved for attention and love, some already broken. And I'll know how to love them just a little bit better because of that old Mama Cat.

The Free-Form Set

One night not too long ago, I was feeling especially lazy. The wrapped-in-a-blanket-with-a-cat-on-my-lap sort of lazy. The kind of lazy that feels cozy, not shameful. The kind that makes everything feel hushed and slow. Instead of sitting primly at my vanity to set my hair, as I usually do, I plopped myself into my squashy, old living room chair. Instead of my beloved round mirror and tidy sectioning clips, I grabbed a handheld mirror, barely the size of a teacup saucer, and used my fingers to haphazardly part off damp bits of hair.

The result was what I can only describe as a "free-form" set. Squished pink rollers jutted out at odd angles, random tufts had escaped altogether, and the usual crisp symmetry of my pin curl pattern was nowhere to be found. I looked, frankly, like a woman halfway through an elaborate craft project who had gotten distracted by a cookie (cinnamon oatmeal raisin, to be specific). But it was late, I was tired, and I needed to get Millen started on her bedtime routine. I left that mess of pink foam and white hair, shrugged, and went to bed.

The next morning, I unwound the rollers, expecting a chaotic mess. And yet, oh, my darlings! There they were. Sweet little ringlets bouncing rebelliously around my ears, tiny but bold spirals doing their own thing. The smooth rolls and sculpted waves I'd intended weren't quite there, but something delightful had taken their place. The volume was exuberant. The texture, buoyant. I looked a bit like a slightly frazzled fairy godmother, and I loved it.

One of the questions I'm most often asked is why I go to all the trouble to roll my hair up, just to brush it out and pin it back up again. I could go into great detail, talking about domestic history and the nuances of 1940s fashion, about my personal aesthetic journey and the evolution of my taste. But the simplest answer is: it brings me joy.

That joy doesn't always come in the neat, symmetrical form I imagined. Sometimes it arrives unruly and unpredictable, in a curl gone rogue or a style that surprises me. And often, the things that matter most to us make no sense to others. When the world is in turmoil, it can feel silly to care about hair or table linens or the perfect shade of tulip pink. But loving what you love, especially when it makes no sense to anyone else, is one of life's quiet rebellions.

Over the years, I've spent a great deal of time worrying about how things might turn out. Big things. Little things. Will we be able to pay the bills this month with only thirty-seven dollars in the account? Can I help my teen through this latest heartbreak? Will the toddler ever ditch that pacifier? That twinge in my back, should I be concerned? Do we need a new porch roof? Does the cat have worms? Does my third grader need glasses? All of it.

And yes, some of those fears came to pass. Some bills didn't get paid on time. The twinges I was trying to ignore turned out to be arthritis. That cat? Yes, she had worms, and yes, she threw up on my vintage woolen hooked rug. But every single one of those disasters, I got through. Every single one. And you, my dear, got through yours too.

You've made it through every terrible Tuesday, every fretful Friday, every long Thursday night when sleep wouldn't come. You've come through messy mornings, uncertain choices, awkward moments. You've come through illnesses, arguments, broken appliances, broken hearts. You made it.

So now, if you can, take a breath. Let go of just one worry today. Maybe things won't go perfectly. But maybe, just maybe, things will turn out better than you dared hope. Sometimes the best curls come from the messiest sets.

Loving what you love,
especially when it
makes no sense to
anyone else, is one of life's
quiet rebellions.

Asking for a Little Lift

Have you ever felt let down by friends or loved ones? That quiet, heavy feeling of disappointment when they don't show up the way you hoped they would? Maybe they didn't seem to notice you were struggling. Maybe they didn't offer the support you needed during a hard time.

Or perhaps you are the one who has let others down. You completely forgot about your friend's surgery date. And that casserole dinner you planned on sending? Also forgotten. You thought your daughter's life was going swimmingly, joyfully living an exciting new phase. But a year later, she tells you how she struggled. And you didn't notice. You fell back asleep on a Saturday morning, and the stray cats missed their breakfast.

People in our lives can seem selfish or distracted sometimes, but often, just like us, they are caught up in their own hard season, weighed down with worries we cannot always see. Meanwhile, our hearts are quietly longing for comfort, for someone to tend to us, to notice.

I have learned that when I find myself feeling let down or disappointed, more often than not, it is because I never let anyone know I needed their help. I held it all inside. I felt self-conscious. I was afraid to be vulnerable. I didn't ask for what I needed.

But here is what I want to tell you: If you ever need a little boost, if your heart feels heavy or lonely, I hope you will be brave enough to say so. Let your loved ones know. Let your friends know. I promise there is love waiting for you.

Over and over again, our community has shown me how warm and safe and generous it can be. It is one of the kindest places I have ever known.

Do not be afraid to ask for love and encouragement, my darling. There is plenty here for you. We have lots to share.

Kitchen Contentment

Once upon a rather stressful Tuesday, I found myself scrubbing the kitchen sink like it had personally done me wrong. Bills were due, the baby was cranky. My teen daughter's hair wasn't cooperating, and, well, it was the end of the world! Truth be told, I was more than a little cranky myself. Even the cat was judging me. Everything felt heavy. And yet, in the middle of all that mess, I caught sight of the afternoon sun pouring through the thin cotton curtains, falling in golden puddles across the counter. There were crumbs, yes, and probably a sticky spot or two, but somehow, in that moment, the light made everything shimmer with a kind of soft holiness.

I've lived long enough to know that beauty doesn't wait for life to calm down. She shows up in the middle of it, spoon in hand, stirring the soup, humming while she wipes down the stove. She slips into the ordinary and does something extraordinary with it, if you're paying attention.

People sometimes tell me my life looks idyllic, and in many ways, it is. I'm content. I've built something sweet and meaningful and just my speed, and I'm grateful every single day. But contentment didn't arrive like a gift at the door. It came after one burned dinner, one overdraft fee, one tearful late-night conversation at a time. It came from deciding to keep looking for goodness . . . even when it was hard to see.

In the hardest seasons, I've found peace in the most unexpected corners: the hiss of the kettle, the rhythm of folding laundry, the comfort of buttered toast on a bad day. I've made friends with ordinary things. I've let beauty catch me off guard. I've let joy sneak in the back door.

If you're struggling right now, my dear one, if you're in the middle of your own mess, be kind to yourself. Let yourself feel it all. And when you're able, look up. There might be sunlight on your countertop, or a bit of quiet between the clatter, or just the sweetness of knowing that even now, you are doing your best.

And I'm so proud of you for that.

You Already Have Everything You Need

Every holiday season, I set up my favorite Christmas decoration: a simple, humble wooden nativity set. Just the infant Christ, along with Mary and Joseph, no taller than a couple of inches each, rustically carved and washed in faint watercolors. There's no glitter, no elaborate finish. And yet, it's the piece I look forward to most each year.

When I first got this tiny Holy Family, years ago when my children were little, I didn't see it as precious. Not at all. I had wanted the larger-size figures—the eight- or ten-inch ones. I wanted the full, elaborate display: three kings and their many attendants, camels and elephants loaded with embroidered boxes of gold and gifts. I wanted shepherds and flocks of sheep, bustling villagers with baskets of eggs and arms full of produce. A whole dramatic tableau stretching across the dining room server like a Renaissance painting come to life.

But I couldn't afford all of that. Not even close. These three tiny figures were all I could have.

That first year, I didn't even use them. They looked so small and sad and lonely on their own. And honestly, I felt the same. It had been a hard year. Inspiration was scarce. Celebration felt flat. Reverence was something I remembered but couldn't quite touch.

Then, the following year, I remembered an old children's altar we had tucked away, a whimsical little thing with carved birds and branches across the top and a tiny light at the back that glowed like dawn. I placed the tiny Holy Family there, in the glow of that soft light, in front of a postcard of a quiet winter forest.

Suddenly, those figures didn't look pathetic anymore. They looked peaceful. Their tininess and simplicity felt somehow sacred. Their aloneness wasn't lonely, it was precious solitude, quiet, safe, and free. My children added toys and bits of snowy lace, and we created a sanctuary for the dear little family, full of warmth and wonder.

And I thought: *Isn't it funny how I already had exactly what I needed*?

I just needed to see my things differently. Pull dusty, forgotten things out into different light. Look at what I have from a new direction. Let old things tell a new story.

How often that turns out to be true!

We spend so much of our lives longing for more—more beauty, more abundance, more confirmation that we're doing it right. That we're enough. But so often, what we need isn't something new at all. Sometimes, we just need to rearrange what we already have. Let a little light in. Clear the dust off the things we've stopped seeing clearly.

That little nativity set has become something sacred to me. Not just because of what it depicts but because of what it taught me: that enough doesn't have to be elaborate. That joy doesn't depend on grandeur. That reverence can be found in the humblest corners, if we remember to look with eyes that are willing to see.

We all have these moments tucked in our lives, reminders that what we long for may already be curled quietly in the corners. That the tiny, overlooked bits can become the very heart of something beautiful. That with the right setting, the right light, even the smallest offerings shine.

When you feel like you're falling short—of beauty, of celebration, of a life that dazzles—pause. Reexamine. Rethink. Refashion. Take stock.

You might already have everything you need. It just needs a little light—and your loving eyes—to be seen.

Failures in Baking

When my brother and I were about seven or eight years old, we decided to bake a chocolate cake all by ourselves. It was an ambitious little endeavor, considering my brother needed to climb on top of the counter to reach the cupboard doors, and I needed a step stool to even reach the counter. But we were determined. We mixed and stirred and proudly poured the batter into the pan. The whole house began to smell like heaven. We waited. We peeked through the oven window, and when the timer rang, we pulled out a cake that looked like a dream. Puffy, perfectly browned, picture perfect.

Then we tried to turn it out of the pan. It stuck like a bug. We had forgotten to grease the pan.

And worse, when we tasted it, we spit it out immediately. Turns out a whole cup of baking soda does not make a good substitute for a teaspoon.

These days I know better. I grease the pan. I dust it with cocoa. I measure carefully and follow instructions in the right order and set the oven to the right temperature. But back then, we didn't know. We just *tried.* And yes, we failed, hilariously and completely. But that's how you learn.

It's easy, isn't it, to look back at our mistakes with a bit of shame, to remember every little flop, and to cringe at the version of ourselves that didn't know better yet? But shame never helps you do better. Shame paralyzes. Gentleness, on the other hand, gives you strength. Gentleness makes it easier to try again.

And that brings me to a story about my biscuits.

True confession: I'm a bit prideful about my homemade biscuits. I've been baking them for nearly 50 years, and I decided it was time to share my never-fail, foolproof method for flawlessly light and flaky biscuits on social media. I set up my camera. After setting up the prettiest camera lighting, I pulled out my jadeite bowl, my tin measuring cup, my sweet little eggbeater with the painted handle. Everything was aesthetically on point. Everything was perfect.

Except the biscuits. Oh dear, those biscuits were anything but light. Or flaky. What is a biscuit if not light and flaky? I decided to reset and start over. Maybe I had used the wrong flour? I had checked, but I wasn't sure. So I tried again. This time the biscuits were somehow worse. Still undaunted, I tried a third time. Now that third batch was edible. Not great, still not flaky, but not a total disaster.

I never did figure out what went wrong. Maybe it was the flour, maybe it was the heat from the lights, maybe it was just a weird baking day. But here's what I do know: Failure is never the end of the story. I went ahead and posted the video, except it wasn't really about biscuits anymore. It was about me, laughing, with the proverbial egg on my face. I thought I was teaching the Internet how to bake, but instead I learned that the most important step in any recipe is gentleness for our own mistakes.

Sometimes, even when we've been doing something forever, we mess up, we forget, we get flustered, we fall short. And that's okay. It doesn't mean we're hopeless. It doesn't mean we should stop trying.

Sometimes it just means we need to take a breath, step back, pause, refresh. Maybe come at our endeavor from a new angle or let it go altogether and try something else entirely.

Failure isn't a disaster. Sometimes failure is the very thing that nudges us toward our next great joy. Sometimes it points us in the most exciting directions. So if your cake sticks or your biscuits flop, be gentle with yourself. Laugh if you can, try again if you want to, or go eat a store-bought cookie and call it a day.

Either way, I hope you're proud of yourself for trying. Because I sure am.

You Are a Blessing

Sometimes, when I find myself in the middle of an especially lovely little moment, I'm overcome with the sense that I've done nothing to deserve any of it. The soft quilt tucked around my shoulders. The warm morning light pouring through my bedroom window. A cat curled on my lap, purring like a hymn. The quiet, gentle presence of someone I love. I've done nothing to earn these gifts. They simply dropped into my days, unexpected and unearned.

And I am grateful.

So many beautiful things have found their way into my life: wonder, ease, moments of laughter, the steady heartbeat of friendship. And truly, sometimes I struggle with guilt about that. I think of all the people in the world who are alone, afraid, aching with worry and dread, and I wonder: *Why have I been so blessed while others must struggle?*

My only answer is this: I don't know.

But I do know that gratitude is the best way I've found to hold all of this. Not guilt, not shame, not a frantic rush to justify my existence. Just gratitude. Gratitude, and the quiet promise to put as much love as I can into the world. To reflect back the warmth I've received. To share whatever I can, wherever I can, with open hands.

You, my dear, are one of those blessings. And I'm so very grateful for you.

And if you find yourself wondering, *Why me? Why do I get this comfort when others must carry such heavy burdens?* please know that you don't have to solve that mystery. You don't have to justify your existence. What you can do is behold your wonderful life with gratitude. Let the quilt feel warm, let the coffee taste sweet, let the morning light fall across your shoulders. And then, if you're able, turn that warmth outward. Offer a kind word. Share what you can. Let the love that you've received spill quietly into the world. That is enough, my darling. More than enough.

Light Your Candle

During the long, dark hush of December, when my children were small, we'd bundle ourselves into scarves and mittens and drive out to a friend's wooded property to gather fragrant evergreen branches for our Advent table: sprigs of pine and cedar, with bits of holly if we were lucky. Our fingers stung from the cold, our cheeks pink from the joy of it.

These days, it's just me venturing out, wearing my woolen bonnet, my long johns tucked into old boots, my clippers in hand as I move slowly through the shrubs in my own little yard. The greenery may be humbler now, the fingers a bit stiffer, but the joy remains. Millen and I light our candles most evenings. Some nights, it's just me alone, striking a match, watching the small flame flicker to life. But even alone, it still feels sacred.

People often say Christmas is for children. But I don't know about that. The magic doesn't leave just because the children grow. The rituals still speak, maybe even more deeply now. The older I get, the more I feel the sweetness of a small, quiet Christmas. The more I cherish the stillness, the glow, the slow unfolding of light.

Each evening in December, we light another candle in our wooden Advent spiral. Just a beeswax taper, rosy and bright, nestled among branches and red berries. A little carved figure of Joseph leads a donkey carrying Mary around the spiral, inching closer to the center each night. It's slow. It's quiet. And somehow, it feels like *everything*.

There is something deeply comforting in this gentle ceremony, this small light cast into the vast dark. And what comforts me most is knowing I'm not alone in it.

All around the world, others are lighting candles too. For Advent, for Hanukah, for Kwanzaa, for Yule. Little flames catching one by one. Circles of light forming in kitchens and living rooms, around tables and hearths. We may never share a meal or a gift or even a smile . . . but we are connected by the light.

Your candle, dear one, warms me from afar. And I hope mine warms you too.

I've come to believe that the simplest things—rituals, quiet moments, small beauty—are what sustain us in the winter seasons of life. We think we need so much. But really, we need light. We need connection. We need hope. And these things don't have to come in grand packages. They come in candles and quilts. In warm mugs of tea. In the stillness of evening. In the brave act of believing that our small light still matters.

If the days feel cold or dark to you, if you feel far from joy or weighed down by all that the world demands, light a candle. Whisper a blessing. Let your own dear light shine.

It doesn't have to be big. It doesn't have to be perfect. It just has to be yours.

Keep putting your light out into this cold world, my dear one.

It's needed more than you know.

Getting Ready for Bed

Hasn't it been a long day, my dears?

Let's start to wind things down, shall we? Up the stairs we go. First I tuck Millen into her sweet little bed, all snug and cozy. Then it's time to turn my attention to the business of bedtime. I begin with something that makes morning a little easier. I lay out tomorrow's clothes: just one small kindness to my future self.

Now let's ease into comfort. I take down my hair and run my fingers through the tangles. Sometimes I do a quick wet set, sometimes just a braid. Then it's into the shower, the steam rising, washing the day right off my shoulders. If a shower feels like too much, maybe you can just splash cool water on your face. Or simply rinse your hands and brush your teeth. Whatever you choose, my darling, just know you deserve to feel clean and tended to.

I do my little lotions and potions, dotting cream gently around my eyes, smoothing a dab of thick lavender-scented balm on the rough spots of my elbows and knees. My nightgown is soft and well-loved . . . though, goodness, I just noticed a few little tears! That's all right, I have time to mend it before bed. And there's something soothing about sewing in the dusky evening twilight of my own dear bedroom.

Now I fill a pretty little glass carafe with ice water and place it on my nightstand. You might prefer a water bottle or a simple cup. It doesn't matter a bit as long as the lid is on tight. You'll sleep better knowing it's there should you need it.

Into bed I go, and I remove the pillows I don't need and pull the quilt up just so. I smooth my cuticles with oil, rub lotion into my hands, and finally take off my glasses.

The window may be cracked just enough to let in a cool breath of night air, or maybe it's closed tight to keep things warm and still. Either way, the room is just how I like it. Just how you like it matters most.

Try to put your phone down now, my dear. Read a chapter, jot something kind in your journal, or simply breathe in the quiet.

Close your eyes and remember:

You are safe,

You are loved,

And tomorrow is waiting, fresh and gentle and full of possibility.

Sleep tight, sweet one. Wake in the morning bright, to do what's right, with all your might.

Conclusion

Want to know a little secret? I've always had difficulty receiving gifts. Sometimes I felt like I didn't deserve them. Sometimes I worried that accepting them would leave me beholden. Other times, I simply couldn't afford to reciprocate, and that imbalance made me uneasy. But over the past few years, I've come to understand something surprising and soft and true: When I receive with joy, when I say thank you with my whole heart, that *is* enough. My gratitude is a gift in return. My pleasure, my delight—they are gifts too.

And you, dear reader, have helped me learn that.

The videos I share, the words I write, the stories I tell—they have always been gifts I send out into the world. Small offerings of light and tenderness. And what I've received in return is more than I could have imagined. You've met these gifts with kindness. You've received them with joy. You've written to me, shared your stories with me, let me know that something I said helped you feel seen. You've laughed with me, cried with me, and told me when something I created brought you a little spark of peace. You have returned my small gifts with beautiful gifts of your own.

So many of the ideas I've explored in this book—the smallest joys, the homely beauties, the quiet sacredness of everyday life—they all lead back here to this: the precious gift of gratitude.

Gratitude, you see, is not just a polite posture. It is a transformation. It changes how we see what we already have. It opens our eyes to beauty that might have been hiding in plain sight. It invites us to slow down, to pay attention, to whisper "thank you" even in the midst of difficulty. And when we do, even the most ordinary things can begin to glow.

The world will always offer us reasons to be wary, to wish for more, to believe that we're somehow falling short. But gratitude gently redirects us. It takes our hand and shows us the soft blanket, the warm cup, the sunlight on the floor. It reminds us that enough is often right here, if we are willing to see it.

My darling, if this book has offered you anything—a breath of peace, a flicker of joy, a moment of feeling less alone—then I am honored beyond words. Thank you for letting me into your heart and home. Thank you for meeting my words with such warmth.

This book began as my gift to you. But you have made it a gift to me.

Acknowledgments

When I used to read acknowledgments in books, I never quite understood them. Authors would say, "I didn't write this book alone," and I'd think, Well . . . didn't you? Now I know better. Writing this book taught me just how many hands, hearts, minds, and moments are woven into those finally finished pages. At the beginning of this journey, the work felt enormously heavy, a burden I struggled to carry all on my own. But gradually along the way, the weight began to lift. I realized it was being shared, quietly and generously, by so many people, each helping in their own gorgeously individual way. I am deeply grateful to every single one of you who helped carry this book with me. This list is my small way of saying thank you . . . with all my heart.

Allison Janice
Amelia Shiffer
Clara Novah
Dr. Vivian McCollum
The entire Hay House team (every dang one of them!)
Iris Blasi
Kate Welshofer
Kelsey Dreisbach
Leon Avery
Mike the computer guy at Hoag Library

Noah Shiffer
Rochelle Bourgault
Ryan Culley
Susan Wiggs
Vinti

About the Author

DIANE SHIFFER is a retired teacher, mother of five, and the Internet's favorite nana with over 2M followers across platforms with whom she shares the cozy, candid, and captivating posts for which she has become well known. She began her career working in day treatment programs for people with developmental disabilities. She also worked in preschools before becoming a special services coordinator for Head Start, a federal program that provides comprehensive services to low-income children and their families. She and her work have been featured in outlets including *CBS Sunday Morning* and *The Washington Post*. She lives in Albion, NY, with her youngest daughter, Millen, in a house built in 1930 that is chock-full of the vintage furniture and décor she adores. Visit her online **@shifferdiane** on Instagram and TikTok.

Notes

Hay House Titles of Related Interest

YOU CAN HEAL YOUR LIFE, the movie,
starring Louise Hay & Friends
(available as an online streaming video)
www.hayhouse.com/louise-movie

THE SHIFT, the movie,
starring Dr. Wayne W. Dyer
(available as an online streaming video)
www.hayhouse.com/the-shift-movie

***

Be Your Own Bestie: A No-Nonsense Guide to Changing the Way You Treat Yourself, by Misha Brown

Protect Your Peace: Nine Unapologetic Principles for Thriving in a Chaotic World, by Trent Shelton

You're in the Right Place: Let Go of the Past, Make Friends with Uncertainty, and Discover the Magic of an Uncharted Future, by Colette Baron-Reid

Becoming an Artist: How to Make Art Like a Human by Embracing Failure, Discovering Your Creative Voice & Finding Joy in the Process, by Scott Christian Sava

We hope you enjoyed this Hay House book. If you'd like to receive our online catalog featuring additional information on Hay House books and products, or if you'd like to find out more about the Hay Foundation, please contact:

Hay House LLC, P.O. Box 5100, Carlsbad, CA 92018-5100
(760) 431-7695 or (800) 654-5126
www.hayhouse.com® • www.hayfoundation.org

Published in Australia by:
Hay House Australia Publishing Pty Ltd
18/36 Ralph St., Alexandria NSW 2015
Phone: +61 (02) 9669 4299
www.hayhouse.com.au

Published in the United Kingdom by:
Hay House UK Ltd
1st Floor, Crawford Corner,
91–93 Baker Street, London W1U 6QQ
Phone: +44 (0)20 3927 7290
www.hayhouse.co.uk

Published in India by:
Hay House Publishers (India) Pvt Ltd
Muskaan Complex, Plot No. 3,
B-2, Vasant Kunj, New Delhi 110 070
Phone: +91 11 41761620
www.hayhouse.co.in